U.S.A. The Republic

~ The Empty House

Compiled and Edited
by
David E. Robinson

Copyright © 2013

Maine-Patriot.com
3 Linnell Circle
Brunswick, Maine 04011

maine-patriot.com

Strange times are these in which we live,
*   when young and old are taught in falsehood's school,*
And the one man who dares to tell the truth,
*   is called at once a lunatic and fool.*

*   - Plato.*

There is no way to rule innocent men. The only power any government has is the power to crack down on criminals.

Well, when there aren't enough criminals, one makes them. One declares so many things to be a crime that it becomes impossible to live without breaking the law.

Ayn Rand, "Atlas Shrugged", Ch III, "White Blackmail"

U.S.A. The Republic

~ The Empty House

Contents

Addendum

U.S.A. The Republic

Introduction

Our Republic is now celebrating the 222nd year of the Bill of Rights to our Constitution. Through the wisdom of a few free-thinking men, we have come incredibly far in these years. Our **nation** has been blessed with prosperity more than any other **nation** in world history. The technology in this country compares with no other. Our leadership in world politics and economics has no rival. Yet all this has happened **outside of the "house"** our predecessors on this continent designed and built.

This fantastic and majestic **political building** which our forefathers constructed with their lives and sacred honor, has fallen into disuse and now sits empty. When it was new, it was the most beautiful **mansion** in the world. There was nothing else like it for it was built on a foundation called the *"common law"*. The walls were shaped in liberty by a unique arrangement referred to as the *separation of powers* and its roof was made of transparent material to let in **the light of the Law**... so all encompassing that it is adaptable to any people, regardless of **color, race, creed or religion**.

Our Republic did not crumble overnight. What took place was the result of a delusion, for people would never give up their liberty knowingly - **only through deception**. Gradually the **deceptive-rot** took hold and one by one the citizens of the house called **"a Republic"** moved out, into a third rate structure called **"a Democracy"**.

Napoleon said *"History is a fable agreed upon"* because he knew that history repeats itself, especially when the history lessons have not been learned nor remembered. Thus our history lessons have fallen into disrepair.

Our forefathers founded this nation because they believed they had a God-given Right to walk away from enslavement to the King. Yet, the very bondage they walked away from has opened the door *for the most subtle slavery this world has ever known.* So subtle is this slavery that the citizens are entrapped by their own ignorance through *offers of enticements* called economic benefits. Acceptance of these benefits sets into operation rules and laws that operate outside of the Constitution. Thus, we have the largest and most unmanageable bureaucracy that has ever existed... a bureaucracy bogged in debt because it taught its people that *government* is the provider and problem solver, instead of *the one people* - the subjects that used to live in that special mansion known as *The Republic,* lighted in Law.

The people's freedom has been lost more because of *what they haven't done* than *what they have done.* In the pages that follow you are going to discover why you are an economic slave and what you can do about it - and about *U.S.A. The Republic.*

Yes, you can move back into that mansion known as the Republic for that is what this treatise is about, finding your *"key to liberty".* Always remember that you are the only one who can take back your liberty. No one else can do it for you. You can and you must act independently of the masses. You and the Law are capable *of awesome accomplishments in liberty*. That is why Thomas Jefferson's statement in the *Declaration of Independence* is as important today as it was in 1776...

"... it is [your] *right, it is* [your] *duty ... to provide new guards for* [your] *future security. ... and such is now the necessity which constrains* [you] *to alter* [your] *former systems of government."*

One man with the Law is a majority.

U.S.A. The Republic

1
The Divine Right Of Kings

Human enslavement has taken all sorts of forms since the beginning of time. The most insidious form is when one individual, such as a king, claims that God gave him the right of enslavement. This is called **The Divine Right of Kings**. At the root of this **assumed right** is basic **feudal slavery**. The divine right that the King of England claimed was the right to have **absolute authority** over every one of his subjects so they could not leave his **political/religious jurisdiction**. That is, the King's subjects did not have **the right to expatriate,** according to his assumed divine right over them.

The American Revolution of 1776 was the result of individuals who believed that the King did not have the right to prevent the people from leaving his **political/religious jurisdiction**. The Revolution was fought over **liberty of choice**. Our Constitution is the **political document** that resulted from that struggle and it guarantees our **liberty to choose** the political domain we want to be controlled by **without compelled performance**. Therefore, if we want to move from one **political jurisdiction** to another, we are guaranteed that right - called expatriation. We are guaranteed the right to change our **political territory** any time we desire.

Few are aware today that their **political choice** has been made for them, and it is a **political choice** that has taken away their absolute rights under the Constitution and its *first Ten Amendments* called the Bill of Rights. They are unaware that they were *given at birth* the economic privilege of *an alternative political domain* - allowed by the Constitution but operating *outside of it*. An *alternative domain* that operates with the same Divine Right of Kings as did the King of England. Thus, the Constitution is operating in an *economic capacity* rather than a *political capacity*.

When we ponder why our nation is in the midst of an *economic crisis* like we have never seen before, we cannot understand that it is *the result of our ignorance*. Ignorance of how *our silence* has given *our federal government and its political subdivisions* (called "states") permission to tax its people without representation *and confiscate their property* when they do not go along with the codes and laws - especially *the tax laws*. Ignorance that has allowed our federal government and its political subdivisions *to compel us to perform* to laws that are *destroying our business* by exacting a fee - *like a protection racket* - for what should be a right.

Instead, our *absolute rights* are now *relative privileges* handed out like food in *a concentration camp*. Instead of being able to stand as an individual *for what we believe*, every *special interest group* has become *our conscience*. Laws and codes by the hundreds are feudalizing *the will to produce* from the soul of *each person* by making him pay for *the failures, inefficiency and greed* of others - called *limited liability*. And still more laws are teaching citizens of all ages *that someone else - Uncle Sam* - is responsible for us *from cradle to grave*.

2
Commulalism Raises Its Ugly Head

The world has always been filled **with people with good intentions**. Unfortunately, it seems that the majority of those **well-intentioned individuals** end up trying to convince **the rest of us** that **their ideas** are the best. The extreme in some countries **results in a dictator,** while in the United States there developed **a democracy** with its **ever present special interest groups** dictating the **conscience of the masses**. Yet, more problems are caused when **good intentions** become **compelled performance**.

As many are aware, **"the road to hell is paved with good intentions"**. The result is always a loss of individual liberty of conscience.

In the beginning, America was a free Republic with vast unsettled wilderness open for anybody who had the courage to take up its challenges. Thus, America became **the melting pot** for religious and social ideals and experiments. Of the many **social theories** espoused throughout Europe, at that time, were three theories that fit the mold for America, all three were **communitarian (communistic)** in nature.

The first **communitarian idea** was set up by the religious sects made familiar by the *Puritans, Quakers, Shakers, Rappites /1, Zorities,* etc. The second **communitarian idea** was established by Robert Owen of Great Britain who was born in 1771, and the third

communitarian idea was of Charles Fourier of France who was born in 1772.

Both Owen and Fourier experienced the vast upheavals that accompanied the French Revolution from the onslaughts of Napoleon. As a result of the slaughter, Owen and Fourier came up with ***communitarian plans*** to transform ***the crises-warped society*** of the 19th century into a more humane order.

In 1812, Robert Owen published a paper titled, *"A New View of Society"*.

His treatise discussed **the formation of the human character,** and he proposed ways of **changing society** from what he called **the poor working class**;

> *"... the society of the poor were trained to commit crimes' the latter resulting in punishment. The rest of the population was instructed to believe, or at least to acknowledge, that certain principles are <u>unerringly true</u> - but to act as though they were <u>grossly false</u>. The result was filling the world with folly and inconsistency making society a scene of insincerity and counter action. In this state the world has continued to the present time; its evils have been and are continually increasing and if we longer delay, general disorder must ensue."*

Owen suggested that **the governing powers** of all countries should **establish rational plans for the education and general formation of the character of their subjects**. Plans must be devised to train children, **which would be taken from their parents at the age of two years**, to prevent them from **acquiring false-hoods and** *deception,* and their labor must be usefully directed upon the communitarian view rather than the individual.

One of his favorite phrases was *"train the young collectively."*

Owen deplored *private property* and he blamed the world's problems of ignorance and selfishness on it. He also disliked *commercial competition. "It creates civil warfare. It exploits the many, and gives to a few favorable individuals, which is injurious to the masses."*

Owen said, *"Without equality of condition, there can be no permanent virtue or stability of society."* Owen laid plans for *Associations of All Classes of All Nations* with a purpose of *"founding as soon as possible, communities of United Interest."*

Owen wanted to *terminate the distinction* between the *rich and the poor,* thereby creating *a millennium.* Owen   proposed not only *a national system of education,* but also *public works projects* designed to guard the unemployed against *the mis-educative effects of enforced idleness*. He was determined to set up a commune, he envisioned, and he decided America was *the ideal location*.

Owen's ideas were put to the test when he established his commune called *"New Harmony Indiana"* in 1825. In a letter to a Quaker leader, William Allen, Owen reveals more of his ideals:

"The United States, but particularly the states west of the Allegheny Mountains, have been prepared in the most remarkable manner for the New

System. The principle of union & cooperation for the promotion of all virtues and for the creation of wealth is now universally admitted, to be far superior to the individual, selfish system, and all seem prepared or rapidly preparing to give up the latter and adopt the former. In fact, the whole country is ready to commence a new empire upon the principle of public property, and discard private property and the uncharitable notion that man can form his own character, as the foundation and root of all evil."

Owen had a lot of problems from the start. A major problem was **poor production**. The **low level of production** was caused by **the lack of trained and competent foremen, supervisors and skilled craftsmen**. His **plan for equality** was failing from the start because **those who were trained** could go work in **the open market and receive more pay**. The first Constitution that was drawn was short lived because of a **crisis of morale**. The land of milk and honey **that Owen promised** did not materialize. **Equality for all** was running into trouble.

"No one is to be favored above the rest as all are to be in a state of perfect equality"...

... wrote a wife of one of the members of the society, but she said;

"Oh if you could see some of the rough uncouth creatures here, I think you would find it rather hard to look upon them exactly in the light of brothers and sisters. I am sure I cannot sincerely look upon these as my equals, and if I must appear to do it, I cannot either act or speak the truth."

Social distinctions and *religious differences* had never been as sharp as they became in the months following *this brief experiment* in forced and premature *social unity*. As the problems mounted, Owen and the people disbanded *one Constitution* and drew up *another Constitution.*

In April of 1827, the "New Harmony" experiment came to a end. However, *Owen's influence in communitarianism* continued to spread from the east as far west as Texas.

In addition to Robert Owen's ideas, Charles Fourier was developing similar concepts. Fourier differed from Owen in that the former believed in *religion and private property* /2, where Fourier had *an opposite view*.

Fourier's work was largely conditioned by an unfortunate event that took place early in his otherwise uneventful life. His father, a wealthy merchant, died and left him a fortune of nearly a quarter of a million francs. However, *all of Fourier's inheritance was lost in the French Revolution*.

Because of this event, he set himself to invent a system of society that would *prevent the recurrence of revolution,* preserve his own *petit-bourgeois class,* and abolish the appalling conditions of labor that was prevalent everywhere.

(This has a familiar *"New World Order"* feel.)

Charles Fourier never set foot upon American soil, but his theories did.

Albert Brisbane was a young American of liberal education and at the age of eighteen, he went to Europe to study *social philosophy*. Eventually Brisbane found what he was looking for in Fourier's treatise on *"Association"* /3, and he promoted Charles Fourier's ideas and wrote extensively upon the subject.

> *If we can organize the townships rightly, so that unity of interests, concert of action, vast economics and general riches will be attained. In spreading these rightly organized Townships, and rendering them general, a Social Order will be gradually established in which peace, prosperity, and happiness will be secured to everyone.*
>
> *The great and primary object which we have in view is consequently to effect the establishment of one Association, which will exhibit practically the great economics, riches, order, and unity of the system, and serve as a model for... and lead to the founding of others.*

Even though there were other *social experimenters*, Owen and Fourier had *the greatest influence* on the leaders of the U.S.A. and its *corporate special interest groups*. This influence figured heavily in the formation of *the Limited Liability Act of 1851, the Civil Rights Act of 1866,* and *the 14th Amendment of 1868*.

These legislative Acts opened the door of *the house called "Democracy"*/4 ... that everyone moved into - *by ignorance.*

3

Democracy and Communism

It is interesting to note that Karl Marx and Friedrich Engles were devoted students of Robert Owen. The **communism of the Bolsheviks** was nothing new. It was incubating and maturing, **in *non-violent form*,** right here in the (u)nited States of America almost 100 years before Russia ever knew about it.

Today communism is believed to have been defeated as the world has turned to democracy. However, is there any difference? In the case of *Smith v. Allwright* /5 the courts said that **"the United States is a constitutional democracy"**. In other words, the court said that the United States ... (as distinguished from the (u)nited States of America which is a Republic) ... is a democracy that is allowed by the Constitution, but is operating outside of it.

This court case is substantiated by the following:

"It is futile is to puzzle ourselves as to whether the American or Russian use of 'democracy' is the true or correct one." /6

"... the first step in the <u>revolution</u> by the working class, is to <u>raise the proletariat</u> to the position of ruling class, to win the battle for democracy." /7

"A government of Russia could not terminate its existence either by dissolution or by merger, for it was a <u>corporation</u> formed under our laws, and its

corporate life continues until the law of its creation declares that it should end." /8

Here we see the *real meaning* of democracy and its **communal governing system**. A democracy is the *opposite* of a republic. However, **you are *unknowingly* participating in a *communal government*** - to the loss of *absolute liberty*.

But the Republic can be restored!

4
Private Law and Municipal Public Law

Let's understand the meaning of *private law* versus *municipal* public *law*.

Private law (non-positive local law) consists of the *principles and regulations* that an individual uses to direct his or her own life... it is also called the *"law of conscience"*... the *personal philosophical and religious belief system* that you use to control your decisions and life.

For example, if you say that you believe that abortions are not proper, then you are verbalizing *your private law*. If you say that you believe that it is OK for you to own a gun, then you are again expressing *your private law*.

Private law's only area of function (*outside of your own conscience*) is in the area of contracts. In other words, a person will always use his *personal principles of conscience* in negotiating with another individual.

An example of this would be the merchant who works out a contract with a company to provide items for sale in a store he owns. His reason for contracting with this particular company is because he believes the items they manufacture should be in every household for health reasons. The merchant's *personal beliefs* or his *conscience* are involved in this contract... as in any contract.

Private law operates *outside of the Constitution* under the rights of *private contract* as stipulated in Article I, Section 10 of the Constitution.

Article I, in its entirety, expresses all of the **private law** that is allowed in the **operation** of the **government** of the several states of the union. Section 8 and clause 18 of this Article states that any **other private law** that is necessary for the operation of the government **for the commercial benefit of the several states of the union** can be legislated.

It must be remembered that Article I is not entirely **private law**. There is some **municipal public law** there as well. This **municipal public law** is for the establishment of public services for **private benefit**. (Post Roads and Post Offices, and Public Laws of the obligation of contracts, etc.).

It must be understood that **private law**, as referred to in the Constitution, **operates in the private sector** as a part of negotiating **bilateral contracts** (*two party contracts*). Private law was never meant to operate **in the public sector** as a basis for controlling **public policy**. Our founders made this very clear. In the next chapter on **roman civil law** you will see how **private law** was made into **public policy** by **entrapment** to produce **compelled performance**.

Municipal public law (*positive general law* in contrast to *private law*) expresses all the laws that **limit government** and maintain the **separation of powers** of the **"states in this union."** /9

Municipal public law is an expression of the people limiting the government for their **personal benefit** and **liberty**.

Remember, **the people are the government**. What powers the people **do not delegate** to the government for its *administration* are retained by them. Public Laws assure the people that their *private rights* of *bilateral contracts* will be maintained, separate from any *government intervention*. The only time *municipal public law* is actively used for *private purposes*... in a legal sense... is when a *private right* has been *violated*. *Municipal public law* is then used in the court to address the wrong and correct it.

> *"The individual may stand upon his constitutional rights as a citizen. He is entitled to carry on his own private business in his own way. His power to contract is unlimited. He owes no duty to the State or to his neighbors to divulge his business, or to open his doors to an investigation, so far as it may tend to incriminate him. He owes no such duty to the State, since he receives nothing there-from, beyond the protection of his life and property. His rights are such as existed by the law of the land long antecedent to the organization of the State. ... He owes nothing to the public so long as he does not trespass upon their rights."* /10

As early as 1782 Jefferson told Monroe that it was ridiculous to suppose that a man should surrender himself to the state. *This would be slavery*... and not the liberty which the Bill of Rights has made inviolable... and for the preservation of which our government has been changed.

Changed from the *roman civil law* to the *common civil law* /11 - see section on *roman civil law*.]

Jefferson said that liberty would be destroyed anytime there is *"...the opinion that the state has a perpetual right to the services of all its members."* /12

The "liberty" which Jefferson refers to is **public law for private purposes** and that "liberty" is self-evident and comes prior to the state, and is opposite to the **"blessings of liberty"** in the Preamble of the Constitution... which is commercial. /13

5

Roman Civil Law

Those who have studied U.S. History from the traditional standpoint do not realize that *there is a lot more* to U.S. History. There is probably more about the history of the (u)nited States of America /14 that you have *not been told* than what you *have* been told.

Take for example our federal government. The provisions for setting it into operation were written into the Constitution, but its *present appearance* and *function* are a far cry from what our founding fathers intended. What has happened to make such a difference from the founding fathers' original intent?

In world history, *religion* has always been *the key center for accumulating wealth* ...while ignorance and superstition promote religion.

Religion has been used by everyone, from Kingly dictators to preachers, to persuade people to give *up everything*... from gold and land to their own lives.

Wealth means power and the *power to get wealth* is religion. The Roman Church discovered this early, and became a *"storehouse"* for the money and property the people were persuaded to give to the Church in exchange for *limited liability*... go directly to heaven instead of to hell. As the people became more educated and saw what was really behind their *power of religion,* the Roman Church fell under greater and greater criticism. This led to the development of a **banking system** to handle and control church wealth, and take the critical focus off the Church.

This is how and why **the Church's influence** has always figured so heavily in the **administration** and **control** of world politics. The Bank learned about **limited liability** from the Church .

If you can get people to **borrow money beyond their ability to pay it back**, you can get them to **keep performing** on the **liability of the debt** without ever demanding the money back... thereby, loaning out **that same credit** to more than one **individual** or **company**. This meant that the Bank **was limiting the liability** of the **borrower** so that he was **not fully responsible** for the debt as long as he **continued to perform** by **paying the interest**.

In this way, **real money** (*gold*) became **paper money** (*credit*) by loaning it to **more than one person**. This sort of commerce was called **"private commerce"**. With the church's control over wealth, **private commerce** became the **standard practice** in world trade **upon the sea**... and **private-international admiralty-maritime law** became known as **"roman civil law"**... as it began to figure heavily in the politics of every city and country it touched through **international commerce** and **trade**.

Of the many things that were important to our forefathers one thing stood out, **to become free** from the control of **roman civil law**.

The oppressions of the King and Parliament, was the reason for seeking expatriation from England and the King's assumed divine right. The **roman civil law** (*also referred to as "admiralty-maritime law" /15, "the law of the sea"* or *"private international law"*) was the result of *private church law* operating for *commercial purposes* in the public sector.

The amalgamation of *civil government and church law* came from three ingredients — *Greece, Rome,* and the *religion* of the Roman church.

The political theory of the first two of these ingredients was tempered to accommodate the third. Its originators were *the first Christian Emperor* (Constantine of Rome) and *the first Historian of the Christian Church* (Eusebius of Caesarea). Through his writings, Eusebius had once and for all established a *new way* to *interpret history,* and his followers applied the *same political philosophy* for over 1000 years.

Starting with Constantine, *religious belief* became as important for the state, as *religious practice.* Constantine was... among other things... *a "teacher of knowledge" about God.* The unity of *a threatened empire* was seen to depend on a *unity of religious belief* among its subjects. In a *theocratic society* it was *increasingly hard* to be sure where *things temporal ended,* and *things spiritual began.*

> *"Where a necessary qualification for citizenship was Orthodoxy in religious belief, it was natural that the canons of the church councils which defined that belief should also be the law of the land. Justinian had decreed that 'the canons of the first four councils of the church ... should have the status of law. For we accept as holy writ the dogmas of those councils and guard their canons as laws.'*

But some emperors thought themselves empowered to do likewise and to legislate on ecclesiastical or even doctrinal matters. Hence there came into existence the collections known as 'nomo-cannones' in which the laws of the church and the laws of the state were set down side by side and compared, though the former always preceded the latter ... The 'nomocannones' and the commentaries of the canonists advertised the fact that church and state went together. The two were interdependent and it was generally believed that the one could not exist without the other... In the last and apparently hopeless years of the empire's existence, there were various schools of thought about what had gone wrong. By far the most prevalent explanation was that God was punishing the people for their sins. This was the favorite theme of sermons in the 14th and 15th Centuries ... The only hope of salvation lay in a return to the faith and practice of the pure, unadulterated Orthodox faith ..." /16

Yes, history is being **repeated** even now as you read this. Guilt and self righteousness compels the **alteration of public policy** in more bizarre ways **by the pressure of the special interest groups of the trust** ... and the **inquisition** is being repeated today.

Church law first got involved with **commercial ventures** when the Roman Church started funding the Roman Army during the time they were fighting Greece. From there it was an easy transition to **becoming directly involved** in the **civil government of Rome** and then **converting the**

Roman Empire (*what was left of it*) **into their own Commercial State**. When the Roman Church set up their own Vatican state they became a **commercial enterprise**. From that point on, Church law, **controlling civil government,** became known as **roman civil law**.

Roman civil law is a perversion of **common private law**. The conscience of **private law** was never meant to operate to form **government public policy**. Private law was always a part of establishing **bilateral** (*two-party*) **contracts** and could be used in government only for setting up **private commercial relations** between government and corporations called **"licenses"**. But the **conscience of private law** could never operate without **bilateral contracts** unless it was through some Trust.

With the spread of commerce, the church's influence and wealth grew. Around 596 A.D., Pope Gregory began to move **roman civil law** into England. Up until that time it had not been a part of the English economy, but Pope Gregory was determined to have his inspiration of **roman civil law and economy** supreme there.

Pope Gregory was inspired with the idea of converting England, not to Christianity, for the British branch of the Catholic Church was already there, but to the **discipline** of Rome. /17

Moving **roman civil law** into England was strictly using a **commercial venture** of the mercantile Church to take over the **economy** and the **country**, and **enslave its people** to the private or conscience law of the Church. The **authority** and **conscience** of the Roman Church dictated the statutes, codes and laws, through the King and Parliament, for controlling human behavior that resulted in the best *economic* and *commercial* advantage for the Church. Anyone who was not controlled by Roman *civil law,* at that time, was considered to be pagan. That is, if you were operating free of the *roman civil law* - under the *common civil law* - you were a heathen as far as the Roman Church was concerned. It was their intent to *enslave everyone* to the *roman civil law* for a *commercial advantage*. By the way, this *roman civil law* was referred to as *"black letter law".* /18

To see how this law is acknowledged, look up the books in which your state's Constitution and Statutes are published. What many have found is that the titles to the first volumes, that cover the Declaration of Independence and the U.S. Constitution and the state's Constitution, are printed differently than the titles to the volumes that cover the consolidated Statutes and Codes of the state. In many states (possibly in all) you will find the titles to the volumes that begin the state Statutes will be printed in black Gothic letters. This confirms the fact that the *"black letter law"* - *roman civil law* - is the basis of state Statutes that dictate *municipal public policy* via the private laws of the public trust. It was this *roman civil law* that had taken over all Europe and England and our founding fathers wanted nothing of it in the "commercial law system of the American states." It represented to them a *most insidious form of slavery* of both body and mind, that is, *slavery by entrapment* through one-sided or implied contracts *that an individual was never aware he was getting into,* until he was hit with *compelled performance*.

Thomas Jefferson expressed his disdain of *roman civil*

law being introduced into English common law in 1760 by Lord Mansfield. /19 In fact, it was this decision that sparked the American revolution. After 1760, Jefferson wanted nothing to do with the **common law of England** because of the way it had been *polluted* with **roman civil** (*ecclesiastical*) **law** by Lord Mansfield. /20

In a letter to Dr. Thomas Cooper in 1814, Jefferson goes into minute detail to show how **private ecclesiastical law** (*roman civil law*) got mixed with the **common law of England**. He outlines the fact that the **common law** was in England 200 years before the Roman Church. In describing when the influence of the Roman Church was included into the **common law**, Jefferson said:

> **"If it ever was adopted, therefore, into the common law, it must have been between the introduction of Christianity and the date of the Magna Carta. But of the law of this period we have a tolerable collection by Lambard and Wilkins, ... But none of these adopt Christianity as a part of the common law."** /21

Yet the **common law of England** did become polluted with the **compelled performance** of private church law and Jefferson's understanding of the problem marked out the path for the **new commercial system of the American states** to be protected from the **slavery of ecclesiastical authority** dictating **public commercial law** (*policy*).

In truth, the **alliance between Church and State** in England never made their judges accomplices in the **frauds of the clergy**. For instead of being content with the **four surreptitious chapters of Exodus**, they took a whole leap of faith and declared that the whole **Bible and Testament** are a part of the **common law;** ... And thus they incorporated into the English code, laws made **for the Jews alone** and the precepts of the Gospel intended by their **benevolent Author** as obligatory only for their conscience; and they armed the whole with **the coercions of municipal law**. Also, in doing this, they did not use the "Connecticut caution" of declaring, as is done in their blue laws, that the laws of God shall be the laws of their land, except where their own contradict them. /22

Unfortunately, because Jefferson saw the tyranny of **private ecclesiastical law** dictating **commercial public policy** and **compelled performance**, he was attacked by the "do gooders" as being a heretic. In reality, he saw so clearly the need for **separation of powers** and how **public law** would be vital for **private use** to protect the individual rights of the minority. Thus he stood vehemently on the ground that **private law has no place in dictating public policy**. Those who opposed his views totally missed his solid Christian principles based on **liberty of conscience**.

> **"The common law protects both opinions** [both his and theirs], **but enacts neither into law."**

Those who did not understand this were the first to promote their **private conscience** (religious) **opinions** into **public law** (policy) - the rope of **compelled performance** that is hanging us today.

> **"All honor to Jefferson - to the man who, in the concrete pressure of a struggle for national independence by a single people, had the coolness, forecast, and capacity to introduce into a merely revolutionary document, an abstract truth, and so**

to embalm it there, that today and in all coming days, it shall be a rebuke and a stumbling block to the very harbingers of reappearing tyranny and oppression." /23

One of the most important aspects of the **common law** before 1760 was that it did not recognize **unilateral contracts** (*one-sided contracts*) where there was **no full disclosure** and **no meeting of the minds**. The right to the **private law to contract** was basic to the **common law**. Those common law contracts always meant that all parties involved **understood all the clauses and facts** and all parties had to **agree by their endorsement** in order for the contract to be valid. **Everything was spelled out.** No hidden implications or strings attached.

Roman civil law relies entirely on **unilateral** or **implied** contracts. This is where one party agrees by the **simple act of accepting the benefits** offered by the civil government. In other words, **the individual has something offered to him that he accepts** - usually an economic or mercantile benefit. The act of **voluntary acceptance** — with or without a signature of acceptance — comes with strings of **compelled performance** attached. This is because the very act of **voluntary acceptance** — **by your silence** — implies your endorsement.

The **implied endorsement** creates a **constructive trust** /24 with the civil government for **your assumed** and **their assured** benefit. This means that **the trust becomes the third party** who dictates the statutes, codes and laws by **its legislature** and we are **compelled** to align our lives with them accordingly, **because of our silent volunteer-**

ing. After *accepting* some benefit under **roman civil law**, and discovering the hidden strings attached that you do not like, **it's too bad, and too late**... *you* are bound to **perform** or **suffer the consequences** of those holding the strings. If you **wrong the constructive trust** that you are unknowingly involved with, **you are assumed guilty of breach of trust** and the **burden of proof** is up to you to clear yourself.

Your job, under the **roman civil law,** is to jump even when you don't have to. Their job - **the civil administrator and their courts -** is to tell you how high.

The **roman civil law** is a perversion of **private conscience law** because it is placing the **private conscience of one** or a **few** over the **private consciences of the masses**. And it is done without the **full disclosure** of **bilateral contracts**. This allows government to always become **superior to the citizen** by binding him in a **constructive trust**. This is why there is no **separation of power,** only one power — the government's power.

The people are **subservient to the government** because they are involved in a **constructive trust** that controls their **conscience** even when they are **not aware of it**.

6

Symbolisms of the Seal

Take a look at *"The Great Seal Of The State Of California."*

This seal is a dramatic representation of how *roman civil law* is the basis of **the franchise** of the *"several states of the union"* granted by the people of the Republic. Each state has its own *corporate seal* and most states use much of the same symbolism. Remember, under *roman civil law* the corporate state is *a diocese* of the **National Church of the 14th Amendment constructive trust**.

Note first the seal contains *a woman seated on a rock* wearing a Roman military uniform holding both a shield and spear. This woman is the Goddess Minerva /25 from Roman mythology. This represents **the authority** of the *roman civil law* founded on **the rock** (church) **the private law of the woman** (*of changing conscience or "emotion" that is not absolute law*), **who is the mother of private law**.

The shield itself has the indications of Roman symbols denoting **further private authority** in the public sector.

Across the top are *31 stars* that represent the 31 states in existence at the time California was incorporated as a state. This also shows the relationship with the other *"several states of the union"* who also base their *civil law* from *roman civil law*.

The word: "EUREKA" means: *"I've found it."* It was an expression that has been said to have originated with Archimedes, a Greek mathematician and physicist. He used the expression when he discovered a method of detecting the amount of alloy mixed with the gold in the crown of the King of Syracuse. Archimedes also invented the *Archimedean screw* or *"water snail"* which, when rotated, will move water uphill.

Because of the *symbolism of the seal*, it most likely represents the moving of the *law of the sea* [*admiralty/ maritime law*] uphill and overland to dominate the *substance of the law* we know as *the land*. It could be saying the same thing by expressing the fact that the *substance of absolute law - gold/real property* - is taken over by the *emotions of private law*.

Note also the *sailing ships* in the water. This represents the *law of the sea* (*admiralty/maritime law*) as the vehicle for *private commercial roman civil law* in the state. In the left lower area of the seal is a *miner digging* and behind him is a *sluice box*. This represents the labor and industrial control by the private *roman civil law*. There is also grain in the foreground as a symbol of the *control of the land* and its substance called *"food"*. The bear represents the fact that the *Republic is still there* - the California Republic is called the *"Bear Republic"*.

7
Federalism

There is no doubt about it! There is an **economic advantage** to individuals cooperating for business purposes and our Founders recognized that fact.

What they did not want was the **compelled performance** of **entrapment by implied contracts** under the private **roman civil law** operating within and between the states.

Their law was to be **civil law** based on the principles of the **general common law** /26 and its **full disclosure** of bilateral contracts. It thus became referred to as the **"System of commercial law in the American states"**. /27

Under our **unique type of law**, our government was to have **no direct contact with the people** - unlike **roman civil law**. The federal government was there basically to oversee the **economic cooperation** between the "several states of the union" - **who were foreign to each other** - to provide for their **common defense** and to work out the **commercial business** of the several states of the union as they relate to each other and world trade, based on public **municipal law**, not private **conract law**.

When you understand the **unstated relationship with the King**, this makes sense.

The common law principles that our forefathers brought with them from England were the basis of public **municipal** *law*. This means that the laws are ***bilateral in nature*** based on a ***two party agreement*** where there is a ***meeting of the minds*** with ***full disclosure***. Nothing is ***implied or hidden*** where one could be ***entrapped*** by a ***third party trust*** into ***compelled performance***. Public ***municipal law*** did not allow the private ***commercial government*** to have any relationship with the individual citizen and his right of contract. This was ***true separation of power***.

Private law, which the ***roman civil law*** thrived on, was the ***conscience law*** of one ***"person"*** (*one trust*) over another without his knowing how it happened. There is ***no liberty of choice*** regarding its terms. The terms of the contract or agreement (*also called **"offer"***) are always based on the personal beliefs of the Roman civil government. The ***"offer"*** is always ***unilateral*** (*one way*) where ***your accep-tance*** of the ***"offer"*** is signified ***by your silence***.

Everything the individual gets involved in, under ***roman civil law***, has implications that ***obligate him*** because of benefits being accepted by ***his continued silence***.

"You have a right to remain silent."

There are always strings attached that are considered, by the offering party to be a benefit. The agreement never has definite limits. What is agreed upon is only ***implied*** or ***constructed upon the circumstances***. The implications of a ***unilateral offer and acceptance*** always create a ***third party constructive implied trust***. This trust, ***being the third party***, is always there ***to oversee*** and ***to exact*** what it deems is due through ***compelled performance*** to the rules of the ***private trust*** that binds the persons who have ***private business dealings*** with the trust.

38   U.S.A. The Republic

There is no **separation of powers**.

In other words, there is no way to have a **true bilateral** common law **contractual relationship** because the government has you in **a trust relationship** that makes your position **inferior**, not superior. You become **the trust** and, therefore **part of the government**, while at the same time the government becomes you - and **part of the trust**. You end up being **your own enforcer** as a **volunteer**. This is why the IRS keeps telling you that **taxes are voluntary**. Your identity is lost in the **trust relationship** due to purely **immoral ideas** developed **outside of the legal system** (*because of the movement away from Law*) because the trust's **chief reliance** is on the **power of the magistrate**.

In order to have a **separation of powers**, each power must have and keep a **separate and distinct** identity.

The people must function as sovereigns. The government must operate only by the powers that the people, **as the sovereigns**, allow. And those powers - **of Public Law for private use** - protect the identity of the people, **apart from the civil government**. **Roman civil law** does not allow this.

The federal government that was set up in the beginning was public **commercial law**, based entirely on public **municipal law for private use**. The federal government had no direct contact with the people because the people had not **contracted away** their Law and its **separation of powers** into a **constructive trust** of private conscience.

The state was **forbidden** to interfere with the peoples' lives by the **constitutional mandate** of Article I, Section 10 which refers to there being *"...no law impairing the obligation of contracts."* The individual owed nothing to the state, thus the state could not interfere with **personal and individual contracts** between individuals.

Federalism, without **roman civil law** at its base (*public federalism*) could not come in to Intervene with private contracts between two parties. However, when federalism is based on **roman civil law** (*private federalism*), where both your identity and the government's are confused by the **constructive trust arrangement**, they are constantly a part of the contracts - **they are the administrators of your conscience via the charitable trust**. Under **roman civil law**, you are considered to be incompetent, **unable to handle your private affairs**, so the trust is involved, **as a third party**, in all your private business affairs.

Under **public federalism** (*in the beginning*), business and economic associations were formed for various advantages. There was no **compelled performance** because all relationships were based on **bilateral contracts** with **full disclosure** and **understanding** by both parties involved. When a dispute arose between parties in a state, the courts ruled **on the contract** pure and simple - **no codes involved, no implications to be explored**. Likewise, when disputes arose between parties from different states, then the federal courts **were referees** helping to solve the problem, and the **ruling was upon the contract** (*with jury assistance if demanded*) without codes, regulations or revised statutes drummed up by a **third party overseer**.

So in contrast today, the substance of **private federalism** is purely the **private law or conscience** of a private charitable trust - private **roman civil law**, of the 14th Amendment, with vested interest called **"government"** - moved into the public arena by the **voluntary** (*silent*) **acceptance** of 51% (*a majority*) of the population. /28

Anytime a **civil relationship** is established, it is based on **implied** and **indefinite** trust principles. The result is a government that has created a **third party administrative bureaucracy** that spends its time **making and readjusting** codes and **revising statutes** that dictate **public policy**. This is in order to continue the **compelled performance** required of the **citizens** (*beneficiaries of the trust*) to service the **public debt** and thus promote the **economic benefits** of the **government trust**. The federal government has become a **massive public charitable trust** that is using more than 200% of every dollar for **administration** and the **"ship of state"** is foundering (*not staying afloat*).

In fact *feudalism* (*private federalism*) is apt to appear whenever the strain of preserving a relatively large political unit proves to be beyond the **economic** and **psychic** resources of a society. /29

> **"I can ... fight this Frankenstein which the New Deal has created and which is rapidly gobbling up every vestige of rights which the people have and enjoy today ... I feel it necessary that the Congress take some steps against this bureaucratic invasion, not only of the people's rights, but of the right of Congress and of every other legislative and judicial branch of our Government. ... You are reducing them** [the American people] **to the status of serfs."**
> /30

Take a look at the Titles of the United States Code. The last time we looked, there were at least fifty different Titles. Of the fifty, only twenty-two are **public municipal law for private purposes**. The rest are simply **private law**. That's right, **private law** that has destroyed individualism and the family unit, creativity and the individual incentive to produce.

Private law has siphoned off all the wealth and natural resources of the wealthiest nations in the world, all for **assumed economic benefit**.

What a shame!

8

Two Federalisms

The United States Constitution starts out: *"We the people of the United States."* This phrase refers to laws that the commercial government of the United States uses, to assure a *"commercial law system in the American states"* without the operation of *roman civil law* except for anywhere the tide ebbs and flows. That is, *roman civil law* is left to operate where it always has, as a part of the *admiralty/maritime* law of the sea, in the seaports.

Only the individual - the *"one people"* declared in the Declaration of Independence - has the power to determine a republican form of government as stated in *Article IV, Section 4* of the *Constitution* by calling on *public law* for *private purposes*. This is why the Declaration of Independence was written first. It was the basis of the *"one people" sovereignty* that then established the Constitution.

Before the beginning of the nation and the signing of the Declaration of Independence in 1776, *roman civil law* was well entrenched in the colonies, because it was the basis of the *admiralty/maritime law* that governs commerce upon the seas, *internationally* as well as in *ports of call*. When our *founding fathers* were planning on a new nation they understood the advantage of *public commercial law* for the economic benefit of the American states. However, they did not want any of that *public commercial law* to be adulterated with private *roman civil law* (*as referred to previously*) with its *unilateral contracts*.

Therefore, they met behind closed doors to develop a *dual federalism* to assure that *"commercial law in the American states"* would prosper without the *compelled entrapments* of private *roman maritime law* that would inevitably continue *internationally*.

They wanted to have their cake, the King, and eat it too - strip the King of most of his power to mandate and rule.

Indeed, the main task was to get those old centers to *surrender certain prerogatives*; and the effect of reassuring them to do that led to *lingering ambiguities* in our use of the term *"federalism"*.

Federalism, in itself, has to do with federal treaties and alliances - their neutral use [e.g. Jefferson Papers, 1:311]. But there was an emphasis, in the 1780's, on the ties that connect those *under treaty - the one union* and *united force*, as in the term *"federal theology"* (*covenant theology*).

Federalists were, therefore, thought to stand for *federal power* over and against *the states*. But in explaining their position, Madison and Hamilton labored in the Federalist Papers to show the states that they had nothing to fear from this *federal central power*. Thus *"federalism"* came to *incorrectly mean*, in modern parlance, *the division and dispersal of central power*.

Those who opposed a Bill of Rights at the Constitutional Convention - including at first, Madison himself - who drafted and steered through the final bill - were assuming that the people were already protected by their states' bills... and that the central government could not reach the individual except through the states, which supposedly had put *impenetrable barriers* around *individual rights*. /31

It is important to know as you read this that Hamilton was the force behind the First Bank of the United States, proven in later years to be a front for the Rothschilds.

Thus our forefathers *clarified* the *confusion of "federalism"* by establishing *two Federalisms* that exist   today side by side. One is the *private federalism* that came in with international trade under *admiralty/maritime laws* based on *roman civil law*. The other is the *public federalism* of the new *"commercial law"* in the American states. This federalism is based on the general *common law sovereignty* of the individual citizen being maintained by *public laws* for the *private use* of the individual to conduct his business.

The uniqueness of our Constitution *allows* this *dual federalism*. It allows citizens the liberty to function within *public laws* and its *separation of powers,* or it allows citizens to bind themselves by *unilateral contract trusts*.

Thus the word *"federal"* in the American states refers to the *dual federalism* defined in *Swift v. Tyson* /32 and *Erie Railroad v. Thompkins*. /33

We must remember that the *state courts* handled *federal questions* in the beginning of the nation. As commerce between the states grew, *Swift v. Tyson* was designed to protect the people of the several states from the *roman civil law* that was operating under *admiralty jurisdiction* outside of the Constitution where the tide of *admiralty/ maritime law* ebbed and flowed with international trade.

Dual federalism was termed by our founders as the

"New Order For The Ages". Today we hear our leaders using the term: *"New World Order"* - however this term is being used to create the *old world order* and its *inquisitions* under *roman civil law*... *based on the 1040 Form of the IRS* properly known (under government title) as *"Recapture Property"* (*postliminy: Latin for "bring home the property"*).

Remember, there are *two kinds of taxes,* direct and indirect. Direct taxes are used to produce revenue for *a constitutional government - public federalism.* Indirect taxes are used for *controlling human behavior - and wealth.*

How *preposterously* the affairs of the world are managed today. We assemble *Parliaments and Councils* to have the benefit of *collected wisdom,* and - *at the same time* - we have an *assembly of great men* as the greatest tool on earth.

Duel Federalisms Compaired

14th Amendment citizen	non 14th Amendment citizen
sustained by	sustaned by
Erie Railroad v. Tompkins	**Swift v. Tyson**
1938.	**1842.**
Individual subject to	Individual subject to
political commerce under	**civil commerce** under
private law merchant.	**public law merchant**.
Public Social Security Trust.	**Negotiable Instrument Law /b.**
Marine Insurance for limited liability required under international law - individual is considered common carrier - all carriers must have insurance to cover costs of involvement in joint venture for profit **/a.**	No limited liability interference. **All debt must be paid.**
A debt is never paid.	
All business and trade over-seen.	**No third party intervention.** **Art. I, Sec. 10, in full force**
Regulated by third party administrative trust who take a piece of the action.	for individual, i.e., State cannot interfere in obligation of contract. **/c.**
Choices based on what agencies administrative rules/code allow.	**Free Enterprise** Liberty of choice in all areas of life without government interference.
administrative democracy "New World Order" based on Old World Order	**Republican government guaranteed to the states** as per Art. IV, Sect. 4.

NOTES FOR CHART, previous page

*l*a. *"A case in admiralty does not, in fact, arise under the Constitution or Laws of the United States."* — American Ins. Co. v. Canter, 1 Pet. 511, 545 (1828).

*l*b. Clearfield Trust Co. v. United States. — 318 U.S. 363; 63 S.Ct. 573.

*l*c. This includes the State of the District of Columbia; D.C. is considered to be a state in international law. — Geoffrey v. U.S., 133 U.S. 258; 105 S.Ct. 295.

9

The 14th Amendment

We have now reached the point where we must bring in the **whys** and **wherefore's** of the 14th Amendment — the key to the **destruction** of individual liberty - **and America**.

Nevertheless: Our government is bent on exporting its **roman civil law** principles to the world... as the **"New World Order"**.

In reality, the supposed **"New World Order"** is not new. It is nothing more than the **old world order** of **roman civil law** in a **new disguise**, continually making and adjusting public policy.

The 14th Amendment became law - private **roman civil law** that is - (*purportedly*) in 1868 - but the stage was set years and in some ways decades before.

Of the various factors (in the **history of the United States**) that set up the momentum for the 14th Amendment, one of the first was that the Constitution stated plainly that, **every citizen had the right to contract away his personal absolute rights**. That anyone could literally **bind himself away from** his absolute rights under the "Bill of Rights" any time he wanted to — **by private contract**.

This was called the **right of expatriation** (*more on this later*). He could operate **outside of the Constitution** by contract if he so desired, **because the law was his**.

However, in the **opposite vein,** he could walk right back into his constitutional government anytime he chose to.

Another factor contributing to bringing in the 14th Amendment had to do with both **slavery** and the **corporations** before and during the Civil War. In fact, the Civil War figures very prominently in the 14th Amendment because it was **used as a cover** for **control moves** going on in the **corporate back rooms** of our nation - especially in the North. On the other hand, the **slave issue** was used as a con **before, during,** and **after** the Civil War.

In 1851, an Act was passed called the **"Limited Liability Act."** This Act provided protection for shipowners whose cargo and/or ship was lost at sea. The shipowners and investors were required to purchase **maritime insurance** so if a loss was encountered it would be easier to deal with if and when the loss was spread around.

From this, inland corporations saw an opportunity to make money **if they too** could have the benefits of **limited maritime liability** operating in their behalf. They saw **limited liability** as a way to take more risk to advance their profits, making their corporation **a king**.

Keep in mind that during this time of our nation's history, the North had become the **industrial center** while the South had remained the **agricultural center** dependent on slaves as the basis of labor. Because the **social issues** of **slavery** had been making more noise, what better time to turn the problem of **_physical_ slavery** into a tolerated **_economic_ slavery** by bringing the law of the sea in over the land. And if a war should result over the **slave issue,** what better way to **strengthen industry in the North** than to use the *economic stimulus* of war.

By pushing the *problem of slavery*, the real issue of *economic control* by the *private corporate structure* could be advanced, *unnoticed* - the *first phase* of a *"bait and switch" tactic*. So with the *culmination* of the Civil War and with the *northern industrial base primed by the war*, the slaves *were now freed* of being chattel property.

At this point, *corporate big brother* made a calculated move. Since the freed slaves, as well as the rest of the citizenry, were ignorant of how freedom is maintained, it was a perfect time to activate the *second phase* of the *"bait and switch" maneuver*. To set a law into motion, with a lot of *congressional fanfare*, that appeared to *reassure the freed slaves* that they had *all the civil rights* of everyone else. Thus came the **Civil Rights Act of 1866**, which was *private non-positive* law.

The basic problem with *the Civil Rights Act* was that it had *no jurisdiction over the*, but the lawmakers made it *look like it did*. You see, it was *private roman civil law* that only affected those who were in *contractual relations* with the *private corporate structure* of the United States government. None of the *freed slaves* had any type of *license* with the United States government so it did nothing other than play on their ignorance and *make them think* that it did something, *when it did not*. It also affected *few of the rest of the population*, for the same reason. All it ended up to be was a law that had a *few citizens* in its jurisdiction. However, *the Civil Rights Act* had a more *indirect affect* on the future freedoms of *everyone*, as we look back.

For those whom the United States government *did affect* - those holding *licenses,* or who were *under contract* with the United States government (*including federal employees*) - it did *two primary things*. The Act took away *__absolute__ property rights* (*in personam*) /34 and replaced them with *__personal__ property rights* (*in rem*) /35 regardless of race.

The Civil Rights Act of 1866 moved all those in its jurisdiction *away from __real property__ law* (*ownership*) and established them *into __personal property__ law* (*possession and use*) outside of the *protection* of the *general common law* and the Constitution with its separation of powers.

The only problem with the *Civil Rights Act of 1866* was that it did not have *enough jurisdiction* over the majority of the population. So Congress began *another maneuver* under the influence of *private corporate special interest*. Congress began to make the Public think that *the Civil Rights Act* was not permanent enough, and that there was a potential that *some other Congress* might be persuaded to *remove those civil rights*. Therefore, the only way to assure *permanent civil rights* for all time was to *Amendment the Constitution*.

The same Congress, *shortly afterwards,* evidently thinking it unwise, and perhaps unsafe to leave so important a *declaration of rights* to depend upon an *ordinary Act of legislation* — which might be repealed by any subsequent congress — *framed the 14th Amendment*. /36

What an *assumed noble reason*. Assure civil rights by adding an *amendment* to the Constitution. *Who would be against civil rights?* After all, isn't that what this country is all about? **So now we have the 14th Amendment.** It is unfortunate that, **as we look back at the racial cover** that was used *to get* **the Amendment into law,** we see, even today, the same **miss-use of racial issues** to cover an undercurrent of **corporate private law** being used in the public sector for **exploiting the people as before**.

The 14th Amendment is a **set-back** to proper government. This operation of the 14th Amendment runs **counter** to the ideals expressed in the Preamble to the Constitution itself. It does **any thing but** promote domestic tranquillity. They (the Republican Party) knew what they intended by the vague terms of Section One of the 14th Amendment. They knew that it could be interpreted to extend **far beyond** the **Negro race question**. They desired to **nationalize** all civil rights; to make the **federal power** supreme; and to bring the **private life of every citizen** directly under the eye of Congress.

This result was to be obtained by **enfranchising** the blacks and **disenfranchising** the whites.

This meant the **death knell** of the **doctrine of State's rights,** the **nationalization** of all civil rights, and the consequent **abolition of State control** over the **private rights** and **duties** of the individual.

It meant passing **the police power of the State** over to the **federal power of the national government,** thereby giving Congress **undefined** and **unlimited powers** whereby it would be enabled to enter fields of legislation from which it had hitherto been barred.

The States of this Union were never sovereign. Neither is the **Federal Government sovereign.**

Sovereignty is now and has always been inherent in the American people.

This would be a different matter if the 14th Amendment only presented to the courts questions of law, but this is not the case. As a rule, when the Supreme Court **declares a State law unconstitutional under the Amendment,** what it really does is **not decide a question of law** but a question of **governmental public policy**.

The primary purpose of the adoption of the 14th Amendment was to **elevate the negro** to a plane of equality with **the whites** and to protect him in his newly given rights. In its attempt to carry out this ideal, Congress was effectively **restrained** by the **Supreme Court**. Consequently, relative to the negro race, **the 14th Amendment is negative** and **non-automatic.** It has failed its purpose because no **federal power** enforces it, and because the Negroes had **not been qualified** to gain for **themselves** the ideals which the 14th Amendment sought to enforce. When they did become so qualified, they had **no need of the 14th Amendment**. One of the immediate purposes of adopting the 14th Amendment was to aid in destroying the power of the Democratic Party in the South, and in its place building up Republicans. This result was to be obtained by **disenfranchising the whites** and **enfranchising the blacks**. It was a **nationalization** of all civil rights. /37

So, in 1868 Congress passed the 14th Amendment which accomplished primarily two things:

First, it made each individual a **federal citizen of the municipal corporation** of the District of Columbia.

Second, it combined the Senate and the House in their function so they are now operating for the benefit of *private commercial law*. Until the 14th Amendment, the House functioned for the benefit of *private commercial law* and the Senate functioned for the benefit of *public municipal law* - the benefit of the *individual* under republican law.

Third, it made each person *responsible* for the *public debt* by making them *beneficiaries* of the *"public trust"* that the 14th Amendment established.

The 14th Amendment was also *private non-positive law* (*local law*) because it was enacted to set up a *voluntary trust relationship* that any citizen of the states could *participate in* if he so desired. Thus, the 14th Amendment was instrumental in shifting the citizenship of each American from being *primarily a state citizen* to being *primarily a federal citizen* of the private corporation of government.

However, the 14th Amendment was a *sleeper* so to speak. That is, it could still only *exercise jurisdiction* over those who *voluntarily* chose to participate.

Interestingly, Congress knew that it was making a *conditional Amendment* that was based on *private non-positive law*. That is, the people had a *choice*... whether they wanted to participate in what the 14th Amendment was offering... or not... otherwise the 14th Amendment would have been *unconstitutional*.

So *one day before* the 14th Amendment was passed, Congress passed *15 Stat. 249-250* which provided individuals with the ability for a person *to remove himself from* the *jurisdiction* of the 14th Amendment public trust *if he so desired*.

The 14th Amendment set in motion a process of taking the private corporate law of a few, namely **big business**, and moving it into the public sector to control the masses, **for the people's assumed benefit**. The **actual benefit** was for the corporations. The **assumed benefit** lay with the people **being members** of the **public trust** and therefore being able to receive benefits from the **trust**, benefits in the form of **whatever care** the national government would come up with, **to provide** for them **from cradle to grave**. Those benefits have come **at a severe price**, since 1868. That price is the **loss of liberty** under the Constitution and the **general common law**. In exchange we only received back **relative rights** (*privileges*) with only **assumed** economic benefits. In reality the benefits have been **curses**!

When our founding fathers wrote the Constitution, it was far simpler to enumerate the **few powers** that were to be given to the **national government** than to list **all the powers** the individual citizen would keep. So when the Bill of Rights (**the first Ten Amendments**) was completed, Amendments 9 and 10 stated what powers the **"one people"** would reserve to themselves.

Amendment IX - "The enumeration of the Constitution, of certain rights, shall not be construed to deny or disparage other retained by the people."

Amendment X - "The powers not delegated to the United States by the Constitution, nor prohibited by it to the States, are reserved to the States respectively, or to the people."

Among the powers **"retained by the people"** one of the most important was the power **to contract for services** or *to trade with another person or persons* and *not have the government interfere in any way.* (Art. I, Sec. 10).

As discussed previously, contracts are also referred to as *"private law"*. This *right to contract (use private law)* meant that two people could come to a *meeting of their minds* and *agree between themselves* for virtually anything they would *both settle on,* and the government *could not interfere.*

For example, let's suppose that *person "A"* has developed a skill through special professional education or on-the-job training.

As a non-14th Amendment citizen he has the liberty to *offer his services for sale* without the interference of the civil licensing authority. In other words, the *licensing authority* and *their police powers* have no jurisdiction over a person *who is not a citizen of the 14th Amendment public municipal trust.* Here is the secret of *true liberty of choice.* Remember, you are dealing with a **political choice.** Making your *choice to function* in the *public law of the Republic* means that the government cannot compel you to be *regulated by the private law of the democracy.*

Yet, there is one very important facet of *the power to contract* or to use *private law* under the Constitution. That is, if *private contract laws* come into dispute in the courts, the contract will be ruled upon *outside of the Constitution.* You read correctly! Contracts, or private agreements, *always overrule both the Constitution and the Bill of Rights.* In other words, *specific private agreements,* called contracts - governing individual circumstances between two or more persons - **will always overrule** the broad and general clauses of the Constitution.

This is because it is **illogical** to allow someone to take a clause out of the Constitution **that was not a part of their original agreement,** and use it to squirm out of the **contractual provisions** while retaining the **financial gain** the private contract may have given him in the first place.

In the words of Supreme Court Justice Felix Frankfurter, **"Equity is brutal, but we are merely enforcing agreements."**

What he means is that when you go to court to dispute a contract or private law agreement that you had with someone else, **the courts are there to enforce the contract,** as brutal as that may be, **apart and separate from the Constitution.**

With the passage of the 14th Amendment in 1868, the stage was set for private law to be used **outside of the Constitution** to **financially enslave** the masses and **destroy the republican union**. The stage was set to move **roman civil law** into operation **within the boundaries of the (u)nited States of America,** contrary to what our founding fathers ever intended.

Note the words of concern in George Washington's **"Farewell Address"** to the American People:

"The unity of government which constitutes you one people ... is a main pillar in the edifice of your real independence, the support of your tranquillity at home, your peace abroad, of your safety, of your prosperity, of that very liberty which you so highly

prize. ... it is easy to foresee that from different causes and from different quarters much pains will be taken, many artifices employed, to weaken in your minds the conviction of this truth, as this is the point in your political fortress against which the batteries of internal and external enemies will be most constantly and actively (though often covertly and insidiously) directed, it is of infinite moment that you should properly estimate the immense value of your national union to your collective and individual happiness; that you should cherish a cordial, habitual, and immovable attachment to it; accustoming yourselves to think and speak of it as the palladium of your political safety and pros-perity, watching for its preservation with jealous anxiety; discountenancing whatever may suggest even a suspicion that it can in any event be aban-doned; and indignantly frowning upon the first dawning of every attempt to alienate any portion of our country from the rest, or to enfeeble the sacred ties which now link together the various parts. One method of assault may be to effect in the forms of the <u>Constitution alterations</u> [14th Amendment] *which will impair the energy of the system, and thus to undermine what cannot be di-rectly overthrown."* [Bracket information added] /38

So now we are seeing the results of the **"Constitutional alteration" of 1868**. An alteration that **"covertly and in-sidiously"** removed the **"national union"** known as the (u)nited States of America: **the Republic**, and substituted for it the **economic slavery of compelled performance**.

Yet the beauty of the Republic and the **constitutional government** our **forefathers** set up can be demonstrated from the way President James Madison responded to a bill that he vetoed on February 21, 1811. It shows how forces of **private religious conscience** were always trying to force their **private law** on the public.

> *"...because the bill exceeds the rightful authority to which Governments are limited by the essential distinction between civil and religious functions and violates in particular the article of the Constitution of the (u)nited States which declares that "Congress shall make no law respecting a religious establishment." The bill enacts into and establishes by law sundry rules and proceedings relative purely to the organization and polity of the church, incorporated, and comprehending even the election and removal of the minister of the same; so that no change could be made therein by the particular society, or by the general church of which it is a member and whose authority it recognizes. This particular church, therefore, would so far be a religious establishment by law - a legal force and sanction being given to certain articles in its Constitution and administration ... as the injunctions and prohibitions contained in the Regulations would be enforced by the penal consequences applicable to a violation of them according to the local law. And because the bill vests in the said incorporated church... what would be a precedent for giving to religious societies as such a legal agency in carrying into effect a public and civil duty."*
> /39

So it was not until the passage of the 14th Amendment that the continual push of private law into the public sector won out. At that point, **private conscience law** of the Roman church **became the national conscience** by way of the **14th Amendment District of Columbia trust**.

Now notice this: In **Wheaton's Elements Of International Law, 6th edition, page 304**, the existing rule as to **freedom of religious worship** is thus laid down:

> *"A minister resident in a foreign country is entitled to the privilege of religious worship in his own private chapel, according to the particular forms of his <u>national faith</u>, although it may not be generally tolerated by the laws of the state where he resides."*

> *"The laws of Rome do not tolerate any other form of public religious worship than what conforms to the teachings of the Roman Catholic church; but the right of any foreign minister at the papal court to hold religious services under his own roof, and in accordance with the forms of his national or individual faith, has never been questioned or interfered with. This is what the Russian, the Prussian, the American, and other representatives of foreign powers in Rome, have always exercised [and still enjoy unmolested]; the freedom of religious worship in the several chapels connected with their respective legations. These chapels, of course, are open to all compatriots of the different ministers desirous of joining in their religious services."* /40

The **<u>national faith</u>** referred to above applies to 14th

Amendment citizenship... citizenship based on the ***unilateral charitable social security trust*** (*religion*) ***of the District of Columbia***. Because it is based on a **unilateral charitable contract**, it cannot be allowed **in the laws of the state where one resides** - meaning the laws of the Republic of the (u)nited States of America.

The Laws of the Republic and its separation of powers are not governed by the laws of conscience or religion. The Constitution mandates that the Republic will not recognize the establishment of a religion - the conscious beliefs of one or a thousand individuals - as a basis for Public Law.

Here is the prescribed separation of power governed by the public **municipal law** of the Constitution of the (u)nited States of America. Religious beliefs are a **private matter** within each person which are not intended to be enforced on anyone else in the Republic. This has been the very downfall of every civilization. Somebody wants to enforce **their conscience** - **their religion** - upon everyone else as economics: the exact cause of the **American Revolution of 1776** and the mess of the nation today.

The **"Statute of Charitable Uses"** (*charitable trusts*) was enforced in the 13 original colonies by courts of the **Star Chamber** /41 enforcing **"Writs of Assistance"** /42 (*such as the demands of the claims of the IRS*) and was the cause of the American Revolution. This is because the Statute was based on the **parliamentary democracy** which received its law based on the King's conscience - the divine right of kings. The **"Statute of Charitable Uses"** never had any force in the (u)nited States until the 14th Amendment re-instituted the courts of the **Star Chamber** to enforce *"Writs of Assistance"*.

For an example of the private conscience law of the church being moved into public policy, note this:

"The Cathedral Church of Saint Peter and Saint Paul, also known as the National Cathedral, seeks to serve the entire nation as a house of prayer for all people. The concept of such a cathedral dates back to 1791 when Pierre L.'Enfant specified 'a great church for national purposes' in his plan for the city." /43

So let's take a look at the text of the 14th Amendment so we can see what is taking place here.

Section 1. **Amendment XIV** (1868) "All persons born or naturalized in the United States, *and subject to the jurisdiction thereof,* are *citizens of the United States* and *of the State wherein they reside.* No State shall make or enforce any law which shall abridge the privileges or immunities of citizens of the United States; nor shall any State deprive any person of life, liberty or property, without due process of law; nor deny to any person within its jurisdiction the equal protection of the law.

Section 2. "Representatives shall be apportioned among the several States according to their respective numbers, counting the whole number of persons in each State, excluding Indians not taxed. But when the right to vote at any election for the choice of electors for President and Vice-President of the United States, Representatives in Congress, the Executive and Judicial officers of a State, or the members of the Legislature thereof, is denied to any of the male inhabitants of such State, being twenty-one years of age, and citizens of the United States, or in any way *abridged, except for participation in rebellion, or other crime, the basis of representation therein shall be reduced in the propor- tion which the number of such male citizens shall bear to the whole number of male citizens twenty-one years of age in such State."*

Section 3. *"No person shall be a Senator or Representative in Congress, or elector of President and Vice-President, or hold any office, civil or military, under the United States, or under any State, who, having previously taken an oath, as a member of Congress, or as an officer of the United States, or as member of any State Legislature, or an executive or judicial officer of any State, to support the Constitution of the United States, shall have engaged in insurrec- tion or rebellion against the same, or given aid or comfort to the enemies thereof. But Congress may by a vote to two-thirds of each House, remove such disability."*

Section 4. *"The validity of the public debt of the United States, authorized by law, including debts incurred for payment of pensions and bounties for services in suppressing insurrection or rebellion, shall not be questioned. But neither the United States nor any State shall assume or pay any debt or obligation incurred in aid of insurrection or rebellions against the United States, or any claim for the loss or emancipa- tion of any slave; but all such debts, obligations and claims shall be held illegal and void."*

Section 5. "*The Congress shall have power to enforce, by appropriate legislation, the provisions of this article.*"

First, let's notice the *italicized part* of **Section 1**. Two important facts are derived from this part. **One** - *this Amendment deals with trust law*. The phrase *"and subject to"* /44 is language that is *used for trusts* which are nothing more than *private contractual arrangements*.

Two - **Section 1** states that you are now to be *firstly* and *primarily* a citizen of the United States and *secondly* a citizen of the State. While outside the 14th Amendment, and under the Constitution, it is exactly the opposite.

Next, notice the *italicized part* of **Section 4**. According to this section *"The validity of the public debt (and all its facets) shall not be questioned"*.

Whether the Amendments to the Federal Constitution have been properly ratified is a *"political question"*. /45 A political question means that its answer is *voluntary*. In other words, the court will *never question* your choice but *it will enforce that choice*.

This is why **Section 4** of the 14th Amendment says that *"the public debt shall not be questioned"*.

When you *politically volunteered* for the benefits of the *public debt* (*unknowingly* or *knowingly*) you became a *"beneficiary"* of the public debt trust. So to then to *question the public debt* would be like suing yourself - which is impossible.

However, another *Supreme Court decision* verifies that you can *reject the benefits of a trust* (*the public debt*) if you realize that *you are not the beneficiary*. /46

In other words... *Is it your will* to be a *beneficiary* of the legislature of the United States? If not, then *what evidence do you have* to show that you have *declined to be a beneficiary*? This is where your individual *"Declaration of Independence"* comes in.

The 14th Amendment is a *private unilateral contract* being used in the *public sector* to dictate public policy.

Everyone born since 1868 has - *by accident of birth* - become *subject to* the 14th Amendment. *"Subject to"* is accomplished through the constructive trust created under the *offer and acceptance* principles of *roman civil law* and all of its ramifications, including being citizens *primarily* of the United States government and not of the state in which you live. *You also have the benefit of being part of* and *responsible for the public debt of the trust*.

The 14th Amendment does not say that *"all persons subject to..."* It says *"and subject to..."* which is the first clue to revealing that *each citizen has a choice* as to whether or not he wants to be *"subject to"* the 14th Amendment trust.

14th Amendment citizenship is such that a citizen keeps 14th Amendment citizenship *unless he voluntarily relinquishes it*... which - *once acquired* - cannot be *shifted, canceled or diluted* by any governmental agency.

Allegiance in this country is not *due to the Congress*, but *to the people* with whom the sovereign power is found. /47

10

Separation Of Church And State

In the *14th Amendment charitable trust* there is no *separation of church and state*. Organized religion is in bed with the government today and they are of *"one flesh" with the 14th Amendment*.

The majority of the public interest of churches today centers on the *social issues* over which the government is developing *public policy,* while the churches are oblivious to the fact that the government is operating as a *charitable church trust*. That is, *the government is nothing more than a <u>political church trust</u> for charitable purposes*.

The reader must understand that *what a man believes in his conscience is his religion*. It matters not whether he or she belongs to an organized denomination. It does not even matter if they believe in one God, fifty Gods or no God at all, *their personal belief is their conscience and religion*. The conscience or belief of a man is changeable. It is conditioned according to where he or she was born, raised and educated. *Conscience is being influenced every day by what one encounters*, therefore *the conscience is not absolute* but rather *abstract*. What one man would decide regarding some incident or happening may not be the same as what another man would decide.

The 1st Amendment of the Constitution was for the purpose of *preventing religion* from becoming *government policy*.

Amendment I. (1791) "Congress shall make no law respecting an establishment of religion, or prohibiting the free exercise thereof; or abridging the freedom of speech, of the press; or the right of the people peaceably to assemble and to petition the Government for a redress of grievances."

However, this Amendment has been *misunderstood*, according to the court cases that have dealt with it. What the first Amendment is about (*literally*) is to prevent an individual's *personal religious beliefs - conscience -* from being legislated into law as *public policy*. The first Amendment says that the government is not to interfere with one's right to *express his conscience* by making any *public policy* based on it.

> *"... the term "religion" in this Amendment refers exclusively to a person's views of his relations to his Creator, though often confused with some particular form of worship, from which it must be distinguished.* /48 *The First Amendment gives freedom of mind the same security as freedom of conscience."* /49

Because of its abstractness and changeableness, *religion has no place in the law*. The Law deals only with absolutes. *Law is based on the unchangeable* just as the laws of the universe express themselves through *unchangeable principles* - movements of the earth around the sun and seasons of year, etc. *Law is man's right to be free to follow the dictates of his own conscience without harm or interference to himself or others*. *Roman civil law,* as discussed earlier, *is the opposite*, it dictates what the conscience of an individual should be obligated to

by way of civil government codes and laws.

Since the 14th Amendment, *religious conscience* has become *public policy*. Contrary to the first Amendment, *one man's or a few men's religious ideas* are now constantly becoming or changing *public policy* because the *public charitable (church) trust* formed by the 14th Amendmen operates outside of the the Constitution.

Any organization that is incorporated with a *non-profit status* falls into the category of a *"church"* and is involved in the *public policy* of the 14th Amendment church. They are benefiting as *beneficiaries of the public trust*. This means that all income received *comes from the public trust* because of the *privilege* of existing in the *abstract non-profit status of the corporation*.

Parallel to this, *all 'for-profit' corporations are churches as well,* because of their relationship with the 14th Amendment trust.

Under the 14th Amendment, individual *"persons"* are put on the same level as *"corporations"* - that are also called *"persons"*. The *"state"* becomes the **conscience** of every member of *its charitable trust* and the *conscience of the trust* is according to the ones who have the greatest amount of influence, or money - *special interest groups* - to sway (*to lobby*) the legislators.

If you are involved in trying to *influence and shape* legislative law - *abortion, gun control, vitamin supplements, etc.* - you are involved in *special interests* attempting to *dictate public policy* by way of the *private religious conscience church* known as the *14th Amendment chari-*

table public trust of the United States - *the federal government*.

This brings a whole new meaning to corporations, doesn't it? So where would you go to worship the *"Almighty" dollar"*? Brings *cities and towns into a different focus as well,* and   explains why they are also *corporations*.

Non-profit groups, small or large, *are dead to the law of the Republic*. In other words, the *"person"* is considered to be *an artificial creation of the state* or *a reincarnated group* of *legally dead people* acting as *one corporate person*. The *jurisdiction* in which these *"persons"* exist is a *religious jurisdiction*. The only courts that *14th Amendment "persons"* have access to are *legislative courts,* also called *ecclesiastical courts*, because they operate in a *papal fashion* - dictating the *conscience of the church* (*the Pope's* - *14th Amendment church trust*) as law.

Take a look at the words *diocese, decease* and *decado*. The words demonstrate the *jurisdiction, the state of existence* of the persons in the *14th Amendment trust*.

Diocese, n. [diocise, fr. L., Gr. dioikesis housekeeping, province, diocese, deriv. of dia through + oikein to manage a household, fr.oikos a house]. /50 Province is also *the district over which the jurisdiction of an archbishop extends*. Hence Provincial Courts, the *ecclesiastical courts* of the two archbishops.

A territorial division or colony of a country.

Duty, power; responsibility; thus it is the province of the court to judge the law, that of the jury to decide the facts. /51

Province, in ecclesiastical geography, usually denotes that union of several dioceses which constitutes an archbishopric; it is often conterminous with several states with an entire country, or with several countries having a common boundary. /52

Decease, n. (deces, fr. de + cedere to withdraw). /53

Decedo (decedent) I. to move down duly, withdraw, retire, `clear out' (with idea of making way for another). a. to retire (in favor of another), to give up rights, possessions, etc. b. to give place, yield to. c. Of living beings: to depart (from life), to die. d. Of things: to abate, subside, cease. II. to go away; go wrong, depart, swerve. 2. Transf. Of duty, faith, etc. /54

Because *an individual is dead to* and *departed from the light* and *life of the law* - (*the trust*) - he has *descended down* from being *an absolute sovereign* into a lessor *law of servitude* to the authority of a territory *overseen by policies dictated by a few, controlling the masses for their assumed best good*.

The *"person"* is *considered to be incompetent* under the 14th Amendment. That is, *incapable of managing his own affairs* who has *agreed to this by his silence*. Silence on your part is assumed to be *your acceptance of the economic benefits you were offered at birth* by the 14th Amendment public trust law.

U.S.A. The Republic

11

Expatriation

On July 27, 1868 - *one day before the 14th Amendment took effect* - an "Act" of Congress was passed. This Act was *15 United States Statute at Large* /55 known as the *"Expatriation Statute"*.

This Statute, though no longer included in the United States Code, has not been repealed, and is still in effect. /56

This Statute is very important because it is the *public municipal law* the individual can use *for private purposes* to remove him/herself from the *private trust law* operating in the *public sector*. A private individual who has found himself *bound by private law* in the *public sector* to promote the public policy *of compelled performance* (*which he did not have a choice in*) can access *public statute law* to move back under the *liberty and protection* of the Republic and its *separation of powers*.

The preamble of 15 United States Statute at Large is unique in that *Congress laid the legal discussions to rest* before the Statute took effect to *make sure that it would not be legally tampered with in any way*. It stands as written and is there for the citizens to use as *public law* for the *private purpose* of moving themselves from one *political territorial jurisdiction* to another. This means that *there is a way out*, at any time, *of any United States government policy or law*, including those of *its political subdivisions*, that is *based on private law*.

Whenever you find yourself **bound by any compelled performance you had no choice in,** you are operating in the **jurisdiction of the United States government** and **its political subdivisions** where there is **no republican form of government** and its **separation of powers**. By applying **public laws** for your **private benefit** you can **break that dictatorial jurisdiction anytime you choose**.

The insidiousness of the 14th Amendment is that even though it is the **private contract law of a trust** it is not a **bilateral contract** where both parties sign the document after a meeting of the minds. The 14th Amendment is **"quasi contractual"** - **it is not a true contract** as recognized in the **general common law** - rather it is called an **"adhesion"** or **"unilateral"** contract where only **one party binds himself**. In this case you **agree to the private trust law** merely **by your silence**. If you do not **speak up to let your choice be known,** the trust will assume that you are **a part of** and **a beneficiary of it**. They will **assume** that you have **gifted your life to the trust** in exchange for **the benefits the trust has to offer**.

Under the 14th Amendment, the citizen is assumed to be a beneficiary because he **has not stated otherwise**. **As a beneficiary**, you are **an outlaw** to the Constitution. You are operating **outside of the Constitution**. While operating outside of the Constitution **you only have relative rights** under the Bill of Rights and the Constitution because **private <u>contract law</u>** takes priority over **public <u>constitutional law</u>**.

12

Public Policy And The Democracy

As long as you are under *private trust law operating as public policy* you are under the *conscience of the few* who influence and make the *public policy of the trust* - for the benefit of its members. These groups are known as *special interest groups* or *political action groups*.

This is why the media reports almost daily that some poll has been taken to see what people think. Under the *14th Amendment public trust democracy* the majority rules. This is why you hear the word: **"democracy"** all the time. It refers to the *14th Amendment public trust* that everyone is a part of *because of their silence*. It tells you that mob rule and communalism are the order of the day; it tells you that *if a special interest group can create enough waves of influence* the trust will supposedly be compelled by popular demand to accept the new policy the special interest group has been promoting. If you are a part of the *democratic trust* you are compelled to *"go along"* - *if you are aware of your options*.

Private law is *conscience, ecclesiastical* and *religious law*. They are equal to each other. Under the 14th Amendment trust *there is no true religious liberty* because *the individual is part of the conscience of the trust* and the few that make its *rules called codes*. In fact there are *no true freedoms at all as listed under the* Bill of Rights. Try saying much *against the IRS* and their *prima donna attitude* and see how absolute liberty of speech is.

As alluded to earlier, *the free citizen of the soil* of each *"state in this union"* is not affected by the *private law* of another individual or group trust unless they choose to bind themselves to it *by their silence*. Silence is slavery *under the principles of roman civil law*. Unless you *stand up to claim your sovereign rights* you don't have any.

Each person must exercise a choice *to be free or enslaved*. The public *municipal law* will uphold your right of choice but *you must make a choice* which the law can and will uphold.

Yes, if your are a *beneficiary of the trust* you are living under an *administrative democracy* (*parliamentary democracy*) - *a communal association* - where there is no separation of powers and *your private rights are subject to the will of the majority*. You have no *absolute rights* only *relative rights*. The codes and revised statutes are for the *general good of the association*. Few citizens of the (u)nited States realize that the *"Republic for which it stands"* is an empty house in which no one lives.

With or without *the check of a dictator*, power has been passing from the *legislature* to the *civil service bureaucracy* which alone feels competent to manage the *complex* and *technical business* of the *state*. /57

Anglo-Saxon countries are taking a place alongside of the countries of continental Europe with a body of *administrative law* and its *administrative courts*, at least in *embryo*. The popular conception of liberalism is undergoing a great change. *Liberty lingers on as a name* but a name used to designate almost the *opposite of 19th century liberalism*; for the new liberty consists mainly in *legislative restrictions* which keep one man from exploiting another man *while the state exploits both*. /58

Take a look at how your federal government defines the difference between a *republic* and a *democracy*. The following was taken from U.S. Government Training Manual, No. 2000-25 dated WAR DEPARTMENT, Washington, Nov. 30, 1928 and prepared under direction of the Chief of Staff.

Under which system do you live?

DEMOCRACY: A government of the masses. Authority derived through mass meeting or any other form of "direct" expression. Results in mobocracy. Attitude toward property is communistic - *negating property rights*. Attitude toward law is that the will of the majority shall regulate whether based upon deliberation or governed by passion, prejudice, and impulse without restraint or regard to consequences. Results in demagogism, license, agitation, discontent, anarchy.

REPUBLIC: Authority is derived through the election by the people *of public officials best fitted to represent them*. Attitude toward property is respect for laws and individual rights and a *sensible economic procedure*. Attitude toward law is the *administration of justice in accord with fixed principals* and *established evidence* with a strict regard to *consequences*. A greater number of citizens and extent of territory may be brought within its compass. Avoids the dangerous extreme of either tyranny or mobocracy. Results in statesmanship, liberty, reason, justice, contentment and progress. Is the "standard form" of government throughout the world. *A republic is a government under a*

Constitution which provides for the election of 1.) an executive, and 2.) a legislative body who *working together in a representative capacity* have all the power of appointment, all power of legislation, all power to raise revenue and appropriate expenditures, and are required to 3.) create a judiciary to pass upon the justice and legality of their governmental Acts and to recognize *certain inherent individual rights.*

(Note how carefully this conforms to what existed at that time **as the (u)nited States of America** and how it reinforces **man's right to make law.**)

Take away any one or more of those four elements and you are drifting into Autocracy. Add one or more to those four elements and your are drifting into Democracy. Superior to all others. Autocracy declares the divine right of kings; its authority cannot be questioned; its powers are arbitrarily or unjustly administered. Democracy is the direct rule of the people and has been repeatedly tried without lasting success. Our constitutional fathers, *familiar with the strength and weakness of both autocracy and democracy* - with fixed principles definitely in mind - *defined a representative republican form of government.* They *"made a very marked distinction between a republic and a democracy and said repeatedly and emphatically that they had founded a republic."*

A French **diplomat, politician** and **statesman**, by the name of Alexis de Toqueville, made the following observation about the **democracy of the United States** when he visited here in the early part of the eighteen hundreds:

"The tyranny of public opinion," de Toqueville argued, *"could prove more burdensome than the tyranny of any monarch. Democracy (communalism) does not guarantee efficient government; it does provide freedom for the pursuit of one's own interest, but subject always to the tyranny that comes from the majority insisting that its values* (religious conscience) *and ideas should be safeguarded."*

Toqueville saw the *new state power* as rather like that of the parent except that the parent prepared the child for manhood. *The democratic state is interested in perpetuating childhood in man.* It would provide for his necessities, facilitate his pleasures, and direct his industry.

"What remains (de Torqueville asked) *but to spare them all the care of thinking and all the trouble of living"* /59

13

Losing the Law

Between 1868 and 1933, the 14th Amendment had little affect upon the general population, because the people still controlled *the substance of their law*. That is, the only people affected by the *14th Amendment relation* during this time were those who *held licenses and contracts with the government of the United States* or *were in its employment*. It was not until **June 5, 1933** that the 14th Amendment *took on a whole new power*. On that date *H.J.R. 192* (*House Joint Resolution 192*) *was passed* and the *American people voluntarily gave up their Law* when they *voluntarily gave up their gold*.

That is correct, *the people voluntarily gave up their Law*. To read the history just after that time and talk to people who lived through it, they will tell about *government agents coming to confiscate the gold that the people possessed*. It appeares from what took place *that the people were forced to give up their gold*. However, that is not what happened. *Going along with the "public policy" of HJR 192* was actually *a voluntary act* - *"and was mutable at will."* /60

Thus the individual was a *victim of his ignorance of the Law*. By *accepting the offer of private credit* the population *automatically bound itself over to the private trust*, now having *gone public* because the *whole population moved wholesale into the charitable trust - by their silent* or *negative acceptance*.

When 51% of the population *volunteered for the private trust* it became a *public trust*.

To understand issues *that proceeded* this *1933 event*, we must go back to *1834* when the U.S. Supreme Court in *Wheaton v. Peters* /61 declared that *there was no federal common law*. In other words, *the federal government was not set up as a "state in the Union" under the common law*.

The states were based upon the *substance of common law* and its allodial *titles to land*.

Allodial means that *there are no overlords* upon the land, therefore, *man is his own King* upon the land. The gold and silver that came from the *allodial land* were *public money used for private trade* between the citizens of the states. This meant there were *no third parties* involved in *trading contracts* because there was *no private enterprise trust* (*such as the 14th Amendment*) *dictating public policy*. Trade among the states, at that time, involved *two party contracts* called *free enterprise*. The commercial trade taking place between the states was mostly *in its infant stages* and was *regulated by the common law*. Yet, the *common law of each colony* was foreign to each of the other colonies *without any standard of trade*. Most of the *commercial* (*politically commercial* /62) *trade* involved *international trade* regulated under *admiralty/maritime law* outside of *constitutional mandates*.

With the *growth of commerce* between the states, there became a need to try and *standardize* some form of *commercial law*. Each state had *its own laws of commerce* as based on *common law* and this created great problems when it came to **which state's laws were to be enforced** when disputes arose. A federal circuit court judge by the name of Joseph Story was a pioneer in trying to form some sort of **standard in commercial law** that would appeal not only to the **federal courts** but also to the **state courts** as well.

When Story was appointed to the **supreme court of the united States** he became the **principle advocate** in the landmark decision of **Swift v. Tyson** /63 establishing a general **federal** (*civil commercial* /64) **common law** so as to create **uniformity** in **commercial disputes** involving **negotiable instruments** in **federal** and **state courts**. /65

The decision was based, in part, on the fact that **gold and silver coins** as the **substance of common law** were being **commercially transported between states**. As a result, *jury trials were possible* in federal circuit courts where court proceedings were strictly operated under the authority of **Article III, Section 2 of the Constitution**.

Justice Story /66 had been aware of Robert Owen's communal concepts in 1833 and the influence it could have on the **loss of gold** as a **fixed standard** in trade. Owen was instrumental in **promoting ideas** of how to move **private communal commerce** into the **public sector**.

To accomplish this, the law would have to be changed in order to obtain the **maximum financial stimulus** for commercial growth. For a man like Story, who knew the **relationship of gold** to the Law he could read the handwriting on the wall. With the **undercurrents of corporate special interest scheming** that started in 1833 Story knew that somewhere down the road the **American people** would *lose their Law*. He knew that this would eventually *allow private law* (*private law merchant*) to be moved *into the public sector* controlling *public policy* and resulting in the *loss of general* (*commercial*) *common law* for those involved. In other words, *separation of powers* would be lost in favor of *private commercial corporate business* to the detriment of the *average citizen*.

Also *in the 1842 Swift v. Tyson decision* Justice Story would *assure a trial by jury* in a civil cause between states even if there was *no gold standard* in the future.

So what does a jury have to do with the *fixed gold standard*?

Gold was the land because it not only came from the land but it was also *transportable real estate* (*portable Allodium*). The ancient common law was based on the **real property boundaries** or *soil* that belonged to a person and anything that came from that ground *or the soil* such as *gold* or any other *precious mineral or rock* was considered to be *the substance of the soil* in the **common law**. /67

Gold in the hands of the *common person* meant that the public *municipal law* (*Public Law merchant*) was *"supreme"* because the *person controlled the gold* or *land* where the *goods were produced*. In the true historic sense of the *common law* the only person who counted was the *land owner*. That is, you were *equivalent to a slave* if you did not *own land*. Also, at the beginning of our country *you could not vote* unless *you owned land*. In a jury trial the jury had to be made up of the peers of the person on trial. The only *true peer* of a *non-commercial* individual land owner under the **common law** was *another land owner*. Land ownership being *based on absolute rights* with *allodial titles* - no *outside private equitable interest* or *overseer* involved.

Historically the *commercial traders* and *merchants* were *nomads*. They were *not land owners* nor were they producers. They made money by trading in the commodities that the *land owners produced*. In other words they were the original *middle men brokers*. When the *fixed gold standard* was removed everyone *was shifted* from the *civil commercial* (*public law merchant*) *side of the law* to the *political commercial* (*private law merchant*) *side of the law*.

Where once you were considered to *control the land* and *the Law absolutely*, now you are considered to be a *non-producing trader* with only *relative equitable rights - land or no land*. The result is that there is no more the *possibility of a trial* to judge the public *municipal law*, rather the *trial would be based on the facts of the private implied contract* in which you were now *assumed to be involved*. You are assumed to be *guilty before proven innocent*. The *roman civil law* makes you *guilty by accusation* requiring you to *prove your innocence*.

Swift v. Tyson has been in effect since 1842. However, the *Erie Railroad v. Tompkins* /68 decision of 1938 also stated that there was no longer *"general federal common law"*.

The *Erie Railroad case* was based on the fact that *it is now assumed* that all citizens in the United States are included in the *contractual commerce* of the *private law*

merchant (through the 14th Amendment and HJR 192) **outside of the Constitution** as allowed by **Article I, Section 8, Clause 18**. The **Erie Railroad decision** came five years after HJR 192 (*the removal of the fixed gold standard*). This allowed enough time to pass so that **when people realized** that they had no **right to a jury trial** they would not panic. The **Erie Railroad decision** was based on HJR 192 because the **fixed standard of money** (*the law of the gold*) **was removed**.

It is now up to the individual to decide **which commerce he wants to be a part of** for it is a political choice.

Do you want to be a part of <u>**civil commerce**</u> with its liberty and freedoms under the *public law merchant* supported by **Swift v. Tyson**? Or a part of <u>**political commerce**</u> under the **private law merchant of the 14th Amendment** sustained by **Erie Railroad v. Tompkins**?

Remember, the courts **will not question** your political choice, but **they must uphold it**. However, **unless you take proper action**, your choice will be **assumed to be** with the **private law merchant of the 14th Amendment**.

With HJR 192, the **substance of your law - gold** - was turned into a **commodity**. That is, the fixed standard, at $35.00 per troy ounce of weight and fineness of your money was removed. Once the money no longer had a **fixed standard** its value could then fluctuate according to **supply and demand** just like any **commodity** (like a bushel of grain). This had the same effect **on real property** as well - this is called **inflation and deflation**.

Money is the only Thing in the United States and the world that has **no fixed standard**.

14

Private Money

You can still function and contract within the money system of the Republic using *private money* because Congress suspended the *"Payment" of debt in Law* by suspending the *fixed gold standard*. Even though one is *outside of the 14th Amendment charitable trust* and not a part or beneficiary of the *public policy of the trust* you cannot *"Pay" your debts in Law*. All you can do is *"discharge" your debt in equity*. /69 Because of this *you are the only one who can determine your worth* and *values in money* and *other wise* when not under the 14th Amendment.

Please note: the explanation of the money system in this section is for educational purposes only. It is never to be used in any legal argument because *the choice of the money* (*public or private*) *is a political question* which the courts *do not have jurisdiction* to decide.

When the *fixed gold standard* was suspended in 1933 by HJR 192 it did not abolish the *standard of the law* associated with it - It was just suspended. That is, *it was set aside* in favor of *another law*. It was a *political decision* based on the fact that the *people did not rise up* and tell Congress that *"you cannot take away our law or our gold"* (*our money*). So, the treasury agents came and *confiscated the gold* (*being the Law*) because the people *did not choose to keep the Law*.

The individual could have stopped that from happening, but he would have had to have made his *legal and political declaration* not to be involved with *private law for public purposes under the 14th Amendment* (*not to be involved with the democracy*). Because the people were ignorant of what was taking place *by operation of law under the 14th Amendment* no one knew how to expatriate back into the Republic Law that was still there.

The *Erie Railroad decision* saying there was no *"general federal common law"* was based on the fact that the man who sued the railroad was an *outlaw to the Constitution*. That is, he had *no standing* in absolute *constitutional law* because he was a *14th Amendment citizen* who could not call on any *general federal commercial common law* that remained in the Republic for his protection. /70   He had chosen *by the default of his silence* the private law of the 14th Amendment trust for public purposes. He could not claim his rights based upon the *Swift v. Tyson decision* nor could he access **Article III, Section 2** *courts of "judicial Power"*. He could only be *compelled* to resort to **Article I** *legislative courts* that operate *outside of the U.S. Constitution*.

The Constitution of the (u)nited States of America uses the term *"the several states"*. This means the *territorial government* and its **Article I** *ecclesiastical* **or** *legislative courts*.

Under **Article IV, Section 4**, the Constitution uses the term *"states in this union"*.

"States in this union" is different from *"the several states"* as used in **Article I** (of the Constitution).

Article IV, Section 4 (of the Constitution) guarantees us a *republican form of government*.

"States in this union" refers to the **public** *municipal law* of the **Republican states** for private purposes while *"the several states"* refers to **private** *federal law* for making public policy (*trust law including the Uniform Commercial Code*). /71

Before 1933, you did not have to call on the *republican form of government* and **Article III, Section 2** *courts of "judicial Power"* because they were automatically there because the *gold was there*. After 1933, you have to call on **public** *municipal law* for private purposes to have the *republican form of government* because the *fixed gold standard* is not here.

Gold coin today is *commodity gold* (*also called "fiat money"*) and that is why it *fluctuates in value* on the commodity market, *daily*. It is not guaranteed by the U.S. Treasury as to its weight, fineness and fixed standard.

As to the 16th Amendment, it has not applied since 1933. Today, the 16th Amendment pertains only to the federated states as *political subdivisions* of the District of Columbia including the territorial islands, *American Samoa, Guam, Puerto Rico*, etc., which are construed as **"(S)tates" of the United States**; not to be confused with the **50 (s)tates of the (u)nion**.

Remember, you are presumed to be a *14th Amendment citizen*, since 1933, unless you *bring forth evidence* to prove that *your political choice is otherwise*. It is all a part of *your express Will*. Silence on your part means that you have **conveyed your property to the public trust** and want to be treated as a **constructive trustee outside of the Constitution**.

The IRS and the State Tax Boards are the trustees of **your estate** because of **your silence**. If you want to get back to **the republican form of law** you have to use the **state probate court** to **sever the trust relationship**. Once the **trust is broken** by the courts noticing **your Will in expatriation** you can **take back your estate**.

The trustees received your trust **by operation of law**. You can only take it back by **exercising your private right to use** public **municipal law**. Also remember that **you are presumed to know the law**. *"Ignorance of the law is no excuse."*

Another very important reason for the courts having to **sever the trust relationship** is to **protect the trust**. If there were no **judicially noticed action**, there would be nothing to stop the individual from **bringing suit against the trust** to receive benefits from it **even though they had never paid a dime in the form of taxes**.

The founding fathers established a **republican form of government**. What is unique about the (u)nited States being a Republic is that we had a Constitution to spell everything out about its operation in relationship to its Citizens. The Constitution of the (u)nited States of America was designed to protect the **minority** from the **majority**.

All other republics fail mainly because **they do not have an instrument** that defines **what the republic is** and **how it should operate**.

15

Jurisdiction Of The 14th Amendment

From the beginning, **federal district courts** had no jurisdiction over **private individuals**. They only handled **admiralty/maritime issues**. **Circuit courts** and **the (s)upreme (c)ourt of the united States** had jurisdiction over matters involving **diversity of citizenship**. That is, matters involving **citizens from different states**.

The state courts handled **federal questions** because of them being **courts of original jurisdiction** over issues that **involved contracts**.

When the 14th Amendment came along, the United States district courts could have jurisdiction in private matters of **individuals involved in the trust** because the **trust and its members** now came under **admiralty/maritime law outside of the Constitution** as did all international trade.

At this point, the federal courts were given **"in rem"** jurisdiction **over the people**. The **"res"** /72 was with **the people** because there was no public debt. The **"in personam" jurisdiction** did not apply to the average citizen because the government had no **direct contact with the people** who lived in the states, until after 1933. **The people lost their Law when the fixed gold standard was removed.**

Before 1933, the federal courts **could not assume jurisdiction over a person**. There had to be some **bilat-**

eral arrangement (*contact/conveyance establishing a "res" or "thing"*) that would have given the court **personam jurisdiction** over the people.

All the changes from **civilian to federal methods** result from these changes - the perverted use of the word **"person"** and the new concept of **"res"**. /73

The **"Law of persons and things"** is the **"law of Status."**

"Law of Things" is **"Law of Property"** - or contract. Any changes in an individual's **standing in the law** are a result of how he unknowingly **allows a res to be formed** and thereby becomes subject to **another jurisdiction**.

There is a difference between **"subject matter jurisdiction"** and **"jurisdiction of the subject matter"**.

The courts have jurisdiction of the **subject matter of the trust res** under the 14th Amendment. But as a **non-14th Amendment citizen**, there is no **res** (*thing*) to which they - the court - can **attach jurisdiction**. However, there are areas in the law whereby you can unknowingly **re-convey** subject matter jurisdiction to the court.

Before 1933, the federal courts did not have in rem jurisdiction to **compel the performance** of the general public because the people had not **given up the law** (*gold*). Unless there was some **bilateral contract involved in a dispute**, the federal courts could not **attach jurisdiction** over a person. The federal courts only dealt primarily in **contractual disputes between citizens of different states**.

After 1933, the people contracted for *more debts than there was gold to back up those debts*. Something like $28 billion in debt with only $4 billion in gold to back it up.

When Congress *suspended the gold standard* the nation was thrown into a *debtor/creditor/relationship* because the *people are the posterity of the country*. They are *also the posterity of the debt* through the *social security system* while under the 14th Amendment because it made one *primarily a United States (c)itizen* and *secondarily a citizen of the state*. So under the 14th Amendment you automatically *became responsible* for servicing the *national debt* in order to maintain the *social security system*. /74 [Review footnote /24 on constructive trusts].

The public debt then establishes a *res* (*thing*) in the District of Columbia and since you are primarily a *United States (c)itizen under the 14th Amendment* you automatically become a *beneficiary of the debt*. The *res* (*thing*) is the *debt* as well as the *subject matter*. The public debt operates outside of **Article III, Section 2** (of the Constitution of the United States). This is why the *whole judicial system operates outside of the Constitution* in that *the system* operates only under **Article I** *as a judicial function*.

Every judge can then (*now*) render decisions *based on his own prejudices* instead of on the *constitutional law of the Republic*. Since the 1938 *Erie Railroad decision* justices have been free to render **Article I** *ecclesiastical* or *legislative court decisions* based on *their own desires or political pressures* instead of on the *Constitution*, and they are *immune from suit* because it is a *judicial func-*

tion - *not a* **"judicial Power"** as in **Article III, Section 2** *courts*.

Under the **14th Amendment trust relationship**, the federal government (*in dealings with its citizens*) automatically has **"in rem" jurisdiction** over all **14th Amendment citizens** (*also called U.S. (c)itizens*) and when the government has **"in rem" jurisdiction** the government automatically receives **"in personam" jurisdiction** at the same time.

"Jurisdiction in rem depends solely on the **physical control** of the **res** by the **sovereign exercising jurisdiction** [*jurisdiction of the* **14th Amendment public charitable trust** *of the District of Columbia*] ... thus where property is carried into a **foreign territory** [*the District of Columbia*] **without the cooperation or the consent of the owner,** jurisdiction **cannot be exercised".** /75 [Bracketed words added]

General jurisdiction is public *municipal law* for private purposes, while local jurisdiction, also called "local laws", are private law for public purposes.

When a person expatriates using **15 Statutes at Large** his **whole estate** comes back **out of the trust**.

So the state under **"local law"** (*Washington D.C. and its political subdivisions*) loses **"in rem" jurisdiction** and therefore **"personam" jurisdiction** as well.

The court can compel you to appear, but it **cannot attach subject matter jurisdiction** because the **subject matter** or the **trust res** is no longer in **Washington D.C. or one of its political subdivisions**. It has been **removed back under the Republic** by your **political Will** - both in fact and in law.

HJR 192 *is mutable by will*. /76

The insolvency of the government - **as declared by suspension of the gold standard** - is not something that everyone has to participate in. Not everyone has to be **an "insolvent"**. The people had put more demands on the **payment of gold** than there was **gold in the treasury** so **the gold standard** was suspended... but the individual does not have to **go along with public policy,** especially the public policy that is a **result of private law** (*private law for public purposes*).

Before June 5, 1933 there was **_public_ money** for **_private_ debts**. After June 5, 1933 there was **_private_ money** for **_public_ debts**. Now all **private credit money** operating in the **public sector as public policy** is all that has been made available to **discharge** (*not pay*) **private debts**, since June 5, 1933. The individual who is a **non-14th Amendment citizen** can technically maintain the **"gold standard"** because none of the **taxes** of **compelled performance** apply to him.

Since June 5, 1933, everything is predicated on **your personal Will**. Through **public policy** and the **silence of the individual** it is **assumed** that he wants to **continue the trust relationship** and so he **must therefore perform**.

Performing to the insolvency means that you must **contribute to the insolvency**.

However, you do not have to stay **bound to the debt of the public policy** because it is **"mutable by will"** - that is you must state your **will or choice** and the law will supposedly **uphold your choice** to make **public policy toward you of no effect**. HJR 192 is an open ended Act. You can participate in the **public policy - that HJR 192 established** - or you can **decline to participate**.

It must be understood that in order to make public policy mutable **by the Will of the individual** a very definite legal procedure **must be exercised** along with the **proper statute law**.

The Statute must be exercised with the **proper legal procedure** to accomplish **"mutability by will"** (*state probate code with* **15 Statute at Large** *and published legal notice by Declaration*). The Declaration is an **express testamentary Will** when it has been properly **signed and witnessed** and then **published**.

Hanson v. Denckla /77 deals with 14th Amendment jurisdiction. The trust in dispute was a **private trust** set up according to **public** *municipal law* for **private purposes** in the state of Delaware **without any third party relationship**.

Prior to the 14th Amendment an exercise of jurisdiction over person or property **outside the foreign state** was thought to be absolute nullity, but the matter remained a **question of state law** over which the court exercised no authority. With the adoption of the 14th Amendment any judgment purporting to bind the person of the defendant over whom the court had not acquired **in personam jurisdiction** was void within the state as well as without — **Pennoyer v. Neff, 95 U.S. 714**.

Since the state is forbidden to enter a judgment attempting to bind a person over whom it has no jurisdiction, it has even less right to enter a judgment purporting the interest of such person and property over which the court has no jurisdiction. From **Pennoyer v. Neff** we come to the more flexible standard of **International Shoe Co. v. State of Wash., 326 U.S. 310,** but it is a mistake to assume that this trend heralds the eventual demise of all restriction on personal jurisdiction of state courts. Those restrictions are more than a **guarantee of immunity** from **inconvenient** or **distant litigation**. They are a consequence of **territorial limitations** on the power of the respective states. However minimal the burden of defending **in a foreign tribunal**, a defendant may not be called on to do so unless he had minimal contacts with that state that are a prerequisite to its exercise of power over him. This means that Florida had no relationship or contract that tied back to the corpus of the trust in Delaware. Therefore, *the 14th Amendment* did not apply, to give Florida any jurisdiction. Even before passage of the 14th Amendment, the court in **International Shoe Co.** sustained the state courts in refusing **full faith and credit** to judgments entered by courts that were without jurisdiction **over a non resident defendant**.

But it is essential in each case that there be **some act** by which the defendant purposely avails himself of the privilege of **conducting activities within the forum state**, thus invoking the **benefits and protection of its laws**.

The **"forum state"** in the case of the **non-14th Amendment citizen** is the corporate municipal city of Washington, D.C..

"Full faith and credit" means that we will recognize **your laws** if you will recognize **our laws**. So in this particular case, the **U.S. (S)upreme (C)ourt** was saying that Florida had no legal direct tie to the **corpus** or **body of the trust** and therefore they had no **full faith and credit** under the 14th Amendment to give jurisdiction to act on.

The **U.S. (S)upreme (C)ourt** based their decision on the ruling of the **Delaware Supreme Court** who had ruled on the **corpus of the trust** and what the intent of **the settler** (*the person who made the trust*) was.

In other words, **the 14th Amendment can work in the favor of non-14th Amendment persons** because it brings **a dividing line down** between **Public Laws** and **private laws**.

16
Your Will Was Probated

It may come as a surprise to you, to realize that *your Will was probated the day you were born*. Yes, it is true. The very day you were *born by accident into the United States* is the day *you died to the Law of the Republic*. /78   In other words, *by operation of law* you were *born into the corporate municipal legislative democracy of Washington, D.C.*. (i.e., *The corporate United States*).

It is presumed that everyone born into this country since 1933 has wanted to be a *part of the public policy of the municipal corporation of the District of Columbia*. This is because the *public trust* was established *by public policy* when the gold was removed as a standard in *payment of debt*. Up until the gold was removed *less than 51% of the population* was involved as *beneficiaries of the 14th Amendment trust*.

The moment the gold standard was removed, *more than 51% of the population* automatically became *members of the trust*. This meant the *private municipal trust* could be moved into the *public sector* to become *public policy* because the amount of the population *volunteering for the benefits* indicated a *majority public desire*.

In addition, the trust was confirmed by the U.S. (S)upreme (C)ourt decision of *Erie Railroad v. Tompkins* in 1938 saying *"there is no general federal common law"*. In other words, *it is now presumed that everyone* is a *14th Amendment "person"* as *implied by law* and that *silence on the part of the citizen* is his *consent* to be treated as a *"trustee"* of the *constructive trust* and as *primarily* being a *citizen of the federal United States*.

Despite the suspension of the *fixed gold standard*, the *path to liberty* for the individual lies in the *state probate court* because the *general common law of the soil* still lies in the state courts.

"In the absence of the gold standard, there is no way to protect savings from *confiscation through inflation*. /79 There is no *safe store of value*. If there were the government would have to make *its holdings illegal* as was done in the case of gold. If everyone decided, for example, to convert all his bank deposits *to silver or copper or any other goods* and thereafter declined to accept checks as payment for goods, *bank deposits would lose their purchasing power* and *government created bank credit* would be worthless as a claim on goods. The financial policy of the welfare state [*the 14th Amendment charitable trust*] requires that there be *no way for the owners of wealth* [*property*] *to protect themselves*." /80 [Bracketed words added]

The establishment of the *adjustable gold standard* will not change the law back to the way it was before 1933. Just because the Congress reestablishes *the gold standard* does not mean that the masses will automatically be back under *public municipal law*. It will still mean that *if an individual wants to be free of the oppressive government of private law*, it will take *his individual effort* to *expatriate from the democracy* back to the *Republic*.

Credit money has value because of the **need of people to obtain it** to pay off their debts **denominated in credit** for which their **real property** is pledged.

Those who **expatriate now** are still under the **adjustable gold standard**. When the **fixed gold standard** is re-established by Congress. Those who remain as **14th Amendment citizens** will still be **14th Amendment citizens** under the **compelled performance of the democracy** despite the return of the gold standard.

It will continue to be **your right of choice** as to whether you want to be **governed by a Republican form of government** under **public municipal law** or by a **democracy** under **private nonconstitutional law**.

U.S.A. The Republic

17

Real Property

There is no reason why anyone should *lose his real property to this communistic system - democracy*.

The reason people *lose their property* is because they are *14th Amendment citizens*. As 14th Amendment citizens, you have only an *equitable interest* in the property. Technically speaking, *you have legal and equitable interest* but you cannot *execute upon the legal interest*.

This is because, as *14th Amendment citizens*, you have *no access to the Law side of the court*. With only *equitable interest* you cannot *prove superior title* to access the land as a *"citizen of the soil"* which is the proper name for a *non-14th Amendment citizen* - or *Denizen*.

It is your *standing in the law* that determines whether you have *access to the law* to save your land or otherwise. This is not determined by the *title to the land* - as all land titles in the *(u)nited States of America* are allodial. *Land titles deal with land* whereas the jurisdiction of the *14th Amendment* deals only with the *person* (*in relation to his interest* in the land) - *not ownership*. A *commercial system* cannot *create credit* against the *substance* of the common law - *the land*. They can only create it *through the person* who is under the *14th Amendment*.

Within the Declaration of Independence, of 1776, Thomas Jefferson wrote:

"... all Men are ... endowed by their Creator with certain unalienable /81 Rights, that among these are Life, Liberty, and the Pursuit of Happiness..."

You will notice that **real property is not listed** as an **"unalienable" Right**. This is because **real property** was the **substance** that made the individual **a sovereign** in America (*absolute king in his own right*) - it was the **common law**.

In the **feudal systems of Europe,** the kings and the church were considered to be the **absolute authority** or **sovereigns** because they owned the land. Jefferson did not consider **real property** even remotely close to falling into an **alienable** or **unalienable Right** because the **substance of the land** is the basis of **that liberty**.

Land could not be **pledged in commerce** because it is **unmovable** (*fixed*)and it is **the substance of the common law**. You cannot take **sovereignty** (*land*) from a sovereign.

Sovereignty after all implies that **nothing can be more supreme** than supremacy, so **supremacy cannot yield its essence** (*land*) **to another**.

However, the sovereign can **give his sovereignty up** by **his choice - as per the 14th Amendment**. The people hold the land. If the land were considered to be a **substance that could be alienated by the government,** the government would be the sovereign or king and the people would be serfs again as in Medieval Europe. Remember, **the land is the law**. He who controls the land **controls the law**.

"The power to alienate the unpeopled territories of any state is not among the enumerated powers given by the Constitution to the general government, and if we go out of that Instrument and accommodate to exigencies which may arise by alienating the unpeopled territory of a state, we may accommodate ourselves a little more by alienating that which is peopled, and still a little more by selling the people themselves." /82

Within the 14th Amendment the people have had their property **reclassified into an alienable Right** as in Roman civil law. The result is that the people **have been sold into the slavery** (*serfdom*) **of the trust**.

Thomas Jefferson said, **"The land belongs to the living."**

When a person is civilly dead to the law, he is as good as being **physically dead - he cannot own property in the absolute sense**.

U.S.A. The Republic

18

It's Pure Law

The question that is often raised by individuals who were aware of the hurdles of the court system is, *"How are you assured that you will be dealt with fairly in the court system?"*

First of all, we know the lower court judges are going to be ignorant of *public municipal law* for *private purposes* or the *separation of powers* principles. They have been born and raised, so to speak, in the trust system and all its Codes. The only way we may get due process is to *appeal to the appellate courts*. In other words, when you deal with *issues of law,* the lower courts want those issues dealt with by the more qualified *higher courts*.

The second question that follows is, *"How do you know the [s]upreme [c]ourt /83 of the United States will hear your case?"* Many may not know that *there are two floors to the [s]upreme [c]ourt building itself*. The second floor has not been used since 1933 when the people *gave up their law - their gold. The second floor represents a higher law*. That *higher law* is being accessed with this approach. Anytime the *higher law* is at issue - *U.S. constitutional issues - the [s]upreme [c]ourt has to hear the case*. There is no option.

Fourteenth Amendment citizens do not have the prerogative of being heard *at that level of law* because they are *operating at law* outside of the Constitution.

U.S.A. The Republic

19

Take Back Your Estate

It seems like if one seriously questions the government's *tax* and *economic policy* or challenges the *tax collecting agencies*, that he will be labeled a *"tax protester"*. Remember, a *"tax protester"* is a 14th Amendment person who is *required* to file a return and pay a tax.

However, you must take aim at the agencies that are *the trustees of your estate* and when you do you will be dealing directly with the *Internal Revenue Service* and the *taxing agencies of your state*. Taking back your estate means *revoking the gift held in trust* - *"constructive trust"* held by the *taxing agencies*. [Review footnote /24 on constructive trusts]

Starting the process of moving your *political choice* back under republican laws requires that you *state your Will*. That is, you must *make a public declaration* of what your political Will is under the Constitution. Do you want to be a part of the *public policy* - *the trust* - or do you want to be able to use *public municipal law* for your *private benefit*. Making your Will known requires that your declaration be specific as to your desire about *severing the trust*.

It is generally recognized that the *acceptance of a beneficial testamentary gift*, evidenced by signing an *IRS W-4 form or similar tax form* (*1040 form*), will convey the same results as *voting you will*. The opinion has been frequently expressed that *renunciation of such a gift*, in order to be effective, must be **expressed, clearly** and **un-equivocally,** as by some positive act or statement of the beneficiary. /84

The following could be **your Will by declaration** and thus **your political decision** to choose the Republican form of government.

Pay attention to the content of this sample declaration. **Content is important**.

Declaration of Independence

I, John [and/or Jane] Doe, in the name of the Almighty Creator, By [my/our] Declaration of Independence solemnly Publish and Declare [my/our] Right to expatriate absolute, [my/our] res in trust to the foreign jurisdiction known as the municipal corporation of the District of Columbia, a democracy, and return to the Republic.

Any and all past and present political ties implied by operation of law, or otherwise, in trust with the democracy is hereby dissolved. I, John [and/or Jane Doe] have full power to contract, and establish commerce as guaranteed by the full 10 Amendments to the Bill of Rights to the Constitution of the [u]nited States of America, a Republic.

So Done this _____ day of _____, 20_____.

Signed, _____

Address, _____

Affirmed and subscribed before me this _____ day of _____, 20_____.

Name of Notary, _____

State, _____. My commission expires, _____

Notary Public Seal,

Publishing your ***Declaration of Independence*** according to your state's ***Legal Notice Statute*** fulfills this requirement. Some states require the ***Legal Notice*** to be published only once, other states require three times, some more, etc.. Check your ***Legal Notices*** in your ***state Statute books***. Note: Some newspapers will want to put the declaration under ***Public Notice*** which is OK.

A word of caution. Some people have filed their ***"Notice"*** in the court without advertising in the newspaper. If your ***state Statute books*** require a ***"Notice"*** to be published in the newspaper and you do otherwise, the system does not have to recognize the ***"Notice"*** - so beware.

You must start your process of ***severing the Trust*** by filing your **Declaration of Independence**. Once you have filed it and it has been advertised, the newspaper will send you back an ***Affidavit of Publication***. This will be one of the ***"Exhibits"*** you will use as evidence to the ***probate court*** of your will.

My Personal
Declaration of Independence

I am free because I say I am free. I did not contract my Rights away. I do not bend my knee to any earth King, nor am I bound to kiss the ring of some Pope. I have no contract with a CEO / President of U.S., Inc., nor Governor. I am not a party to their Constitutions. I am not named in their statutes. My freedom is not dependent on any government benefit or piece of legislation advanced by scheme & fraud of enticement. My rights are long antecedent to the creations of the State and my Rights are inherent in the fact that I was born a sovereign as bestowed by my Creator... not government! My rights are not theirs to give away, alter, restrict, or diminish in any way. My rights cannot be waived under any circumstance, act, or what I may have been forced to sign in the past. I do not agree nor consent to the trickery, lies, and deceptions of so-called government to subjugate me or my Rights. I reserve all of my rights at all times and I waive none of my rights at any time, and I will not sign anything so that they can steal my security interest... as the beneficiary of my Estate.

A Free Man/Woman upon the Land Land

U.S.A. The Republic

20

What Have You Lost Or Gained?

In the 14th Amendment trust, you were offered benefits. When you move back to the Republic you lose those benefits and you gain freedom. Here are a few examples.

LOSES:	GAINS:
1. Relative property rights;	**1.** Absolute property rights;
2. Compelled performance;	**2.** True liberty to volunteer;
3. Guilty until proved innocent;	**3.** Innocent until proved guilty;
4. Social Security protection;	**4.** Develop own security;
5. All government aid;	**5.** Pursue interests without interference;
6. Government supervision;	**6.** Develop own standards; Only direct taxes;
7. Indirect Taxes;	**7.** Truer value to every dollar one earns from financial pursuits;
8. Licenses.	**8.** Full right to contract with anyone for anything without licenses.

U.S.A. The Republic

21

Be Your Own Lawyer

Did you know that your state's Attorney General's office is not within the true government (*non-commercial*) complex? In fact, you may find it housed with the tax collecting and enforcing agencies. This is because they are there only to handle *private law* for public *commercial purposes*.

This is why all attorneys have the title *"attorney at law"*. They are only licensed to practice *private law* for public *commercial purposes*.

Only the individual, as a *non-14th Amendment citizen*, can be a private *attorney "in law"*. /85 This is because you, as the governed, *control the absolute law* when in the Republic. You can exercise control over the grant that authorizes those who have the *privilege - franchise -* to use private **"at law"** /86 and its *equity* for public *commercial purposes*. In other words, the individual has the power, *as a citizen of the Republic*, to torpedo and destroy private *commercial law ventures* that are being misused for public *commercial purposes* to his or her detriment.

We are each personally obligated by the *Declaration of Independence* to individually challenge *unjust private law* making *unjust commercial policy* that violates our personal liberty. When we all personally and individually gain the   inspiration of the *Declaration of Independence*, as the early citizenry of this country did, *we will each see*...

"... a long train of abuses and usurpations ... to reduce them [us] under absolute despotism, it is their [our] right, it is their [our] duty, to throw off such government, and to provide new guards for their [our] future security. ... to alter their [our] former systems of government."

Each of us functioning in this individual capacity can act as a majority to destroy the *"despotism"* of *private law operating as public policy* opposing our *absolute freedoms*.

In the Republic, the majority does not rule - *the individual rules*. The Constitution is designed to protect the *minority* from the *majority* because it provides for the private individual to use *public laws* to protect his *personal belief system* from that of the *majority*.

If you decide to pursue *expatriation* by using *15 Statute at Large* and *filing your declaration*, you need to be aware that you cannot use *as precedent* the fact that others have done so before you. In other words, you cannot use the fact that *someone else has expatriated through the probate court to have their trust under the 14th Amendment severed*, as a reason why the court should act on *your behalf*. Each case is *individual and separate*, and is based on *pure statute case law*. What Joe Blow does *has no bearing* on your case in the court.

What's more: Licensed lawyers are not going to be of any help. Typically, they are only familiar with *pleading the codes* under the *14th Amendment*. In fact their title

"Attorney _at_ Law" says it all. This means that they are licensed to practice within **private commercial law**.

They can only function in **Article I Courts _at_ Law**. Few attorneys will even **understand this subject** because **they are taught in law school** that the **state is sovereign**.

U.S.A. The Republic

22

The Constitution

As a political document, the U.S. Constitution is little read and poorly understood. Yet it outlines the *incredible ways* that a *truly free people* can obtain and retain liberty. Unless certain aspects of its *structure and meaning* are understood *it will be impossible* to realize the *true genius of the document* that reveals the *pure principles of liberty*.

The Constitution embraces *two systems* of law.

<u>First</u>, public *municipal law* for *private purposes* operating *in personam* (*in and for the individual*).

<u>Second</u>, private *federal law* for *public purposes* operating *in rem* (*in and for property* or any *thing*).

What is hard to at first understand is that *the men who wrote this document wrote it in such a way that it would allow for the very things that government is doing today that we detest so much*.

All of the despicable Regulations and *interferences of "big brother"*, with his detested heavy-handed tactics, are all properly allowed by our Constitution today. *They are perfectly legal*. This is because the United States government is allowed to operate *outside of the Constitution* because it is operating in private *roman civil law*. It is not treasonous for the United States government to carry on the way it does, but *it is treasonous* that the citizenry are *ignorant of their republican rights* that can keep the **government in check** by removing the **roman civil law.**

Of the **two systems of law** that the Constitution *embraces,* the *entire population* have been *herded over the years* into only *operating* in the **private unilateral contract** side. This is the side where we have **unknowingly volunteered** into *giving up* the *part of the Constitution* that was designed **to keep the private law** out of **public policy** when *used, accessed,* and *maintained by the people.*

It is unfortunate is that the citizen continues **to assume that** *voting* **is making his** *desires known* and that the government has *his individual interests* in mind. All the time *unaware* that the government is there **for the business interests of private corporations** because the house of the Republic *of the [u]nited States of America,* - ignorantly vacated, - *remains empty.*

The following Table is an attempt to contrast the Two Sides to the Constitution and how you are affected by them when you are *operating* in that area. The statements are intended to be *self- explanatory.* This table may form the basis of *seminar discussions* on moving yourself back into the Republic.

THE TWO SIDES TO THE CONSTITUTION

Political Constitution	Economic Constitution
Statutes at Large (positive law)	**Code Pleading** (non positive law)
Bill of Rights	**Amendments 11 to 25**
"in Law" ("in jure" = in law by right)	**"at law"**
Article III Courts of judicial Power in Law and Equity	**Article I Courts** also called Territorial Courts - referred to as Legislative or Ecclesiastical Courts
Law of land	**Law of sea**
Negotiable Instrument Law all debt must be paid	**Limited liability** maritime venture for payment of debt
Statutes **public municipal law** for private purposes acts on person "in personam"	**Revised Statutes** **private national law** for public purposes acts on the "res" (the thing) "in rem."
de jure government (inside Constitution)	**de facto government** (outside Constitution) Art. I, Sec. 8, Cl. 18

General Law	Local Law
Sustained by	Sustained by
"Swift v. Tyson"	*"Erie RR v. Tomkins"*
Gold Standard	**Uniform Commercial Code**

Public Law Merchant uses	**Private Merchant**
no inflation	uses inflation to fund growth
true productivity	false production
Prices at par value	No fixed standard

Bilateral Contracts	**Unilateral Contracts**
Where there is a meeting of the minds	Trust Law implied
Two party transaction	Where there is a silent third party involved in compelling
No compelled performance	performance

Common Civil Law	**Roman Civil Law**
jus non scriptum	Admiralty-Maritime Privilege
	jus pontificum fas
	(ecclesiastical church law)

Absolute Rights	**Relative Rights**
title to self and property.	to self and property.
Substance of Public Law	Substance of private law
is the rights of man	is the conscience of trust

Operates under Art. IV, Sec. 4	**Operates under Art. I, Sec. 8, Cl. 4**
"No corruption of blood"	private implied contracts
no interferance with estate	can interfere with estate

Non-14th Amendment individual	14th Amendment "person"
Private individual	Individual considered commercial person "goods in commerce" for servicing public debt Also referred to by state as "human resource."
Freedom of conscience of individual, beholding to no one	Freedom of conscience as long as it agrees with the majority or the masses
Democratic Republic "states in this union"	Admin. Democracy "several states of the union"
"the" territory	"a" territory
Separation of Powers (separation of church and state)	No separation of powers (no separation of church and state)
No communal relationship	Confederacy under Articles of Confederation and N.W. Ordinance
Direct Taxes	Indirect Taxes
15 Statue at Large keeps federal courts from taking jurisdiction	Courts take jurisdiction through 14th Amendment until one proves otherwise

Courts cannot take judicial notice of 14th Amendment	Codes are streamlined private interpretation of statutes at large for public purpose. Codes allow the courts to take judicial notice of 14th Amendment. Codes apply to anyone who has not made a public notice of his political choice (Will) by declaration
Doctrine of compliments Special individualism	**Unisex** No individualism
Innocent until proved guilty Burden of proof rests with the accuser	**Guilty until proved innocent** Burden of proof rest with the accused
Plead to the Law or Statute for defense Law awards damages and Equity on this side Compels performance of award	**Res judicata** judgment bases on merits of case and legal precedence. Courts tell what is the intent of legislation Issue already decided have no legal recourse

Fixed in place and time	Twilight Zone, Quasi Law
as in permanent domicile or resident	No time and place
	Only exists in abstract space
Real-substance matter and content	Artificial-abstract false and theoretical
Heart-Soul-Spirit	Conscience, Changeable
Individual incentive	**No initiative**
true production.	no true production.

U.S.A. The Republic

23

Political Action Groups

If you are trying to be involved in shaping public policy, you are trying to use private law for public purposes or **private church law** to manipulate **public commercial policy**.

No one really wants to have a church or another individual, **without the option of choice**, dictate what he should think or do. Yet what is happening with **special interest groups** is just that. **Political action groups**, also called special interest groups, i.e, *environmental, health, labor, industrial associations, state, county/borough/city coalitions, religious foundations,* etc., are nothing more than **individuals who have banded together because of a common belief of conscience**. Their endeavor is **to put pressure on the lawmakers** of the 14th Amendment trust to pass laws that *favor their beliefs.* If they are successful, then the **laws that result become the policy of the trust** that bind the rest of the 14th Amendment *trust* **beneficiaries** whether they like it or not. If they don't, then *another special interest group is formed* to try and counter the previous one and so it goes **ad nauseam**. The politicians become the pawns of the most powerful **special interest groups**.

The only way to **change public policy** is to prevent private law from having any part in making public policy. This can only be accomplished by each individual acting separately and independently using public laws for *private purposes*.

The only way the individual can do this is to *move out* of the *public charitable religious trust* that is making the public policy and *take back his estate* into his absolute control. Remember, public laws are laws that guarantee *separation of powers* so that *private conscience laws* cannot dictate public policy. All political action groups have failed to make any difference because of their inability to recognize that *our nation was established* - first and foremost - as *an assembly of individuals acting independently in their own best interest* without harm to another - basic general common law.

Even if *political action groups* were to foster a *constitutional convention* the basic Constitution could not be changed.

What the citizen is unaware of is that the first ten Amendments to the Constitution, called the Bill of Rights, were passed as *public in-law Amendments* by the *"states in this union"* known as the Republic of the [u]nited States of America. These do not apply to the "several states" that are *political subdivisions* of the "territory" of the 14th Amendment trust of the District of Columbia - called the "democracy".

In the opposite vein, Amendments 11 through 25 were passed as *private at-law Amendments* by the *"several states"* operating as *political subdivisions of the trust* that have *no application to the Republic and its citizens*. Amendments 11 through 25 function *outside of the Constitution*. Any additional Amendments that would be added by a **constitutional convention** would be added as **more private law only** by the "several states" as a "democracy" outside of the Republic and its Constitution. The **more Amendments** the *democracy* wants to add will not *give more freedom and rights,* on the contrary, only **more oppression and control**.

Any **special interest group** who says that the Constitution is going to be **changed and/or repudiated** in the future **does not understand** what they are talking about.

First, because the **repudiation of the Constitution was started in 1868** by the passage of the 14th Amendment **and completed** by the people *giving up their law (gold) in 1933* - to move *out from under the Republic* and its *constitutionally protected rights* **into parliamentary democracy**...

Second, because the basic **Constitution of the Republic** can be changed **only by the people of the Republic** and there is **nobody living there now**. The only changes to the Constitution that **the 14th Amendment democracy trust and its political interest groups** can make for its citizens and itself - only comes with **more oppression and control**.

As long as **the people of the democracy** continue to function under the **group mentality** (*based on the mob rule of opinion polls under the* Roman *civil law*) more and more demands are put on the **private commercial system**. The more *claims for benefits* from the system, the **greater the tyranny and oppression required** to make the people *perform to the debt and the interest on the debt that is created to supply the peoples' demands.*

It is the debt and its **uncontrolled interest**, that is causing the production of the American worker to come to a halt. He is being taxed in **ever increasing amounts and ways** to pay for the **federal debt** he has **unknowingly and voluntarily demanded by his silence** - a silence that is financing **his destruction!**

Government produces nothing... it can only take away. Why can't the people see that the **same thing is happening in the government today** that happened in those 147 communistic/social experiments in the early days of our country? The non- producers overwhelmed the producers to cause a **total collapse** of the commune.

It is bizarre how the people of our nation sense that **something is drastically wrong** both politically and economically, and yet keep making all manner of beneficial claims (*now they are pushing for national health insurance*) **the very cause of our national economical illness**. It seems that **no none can see the forest for the trees**.

No one can see that they must **unequivocally stop all demands from the government** and become self-sufficient at all cost. When individuals change their **standing in the law** from 14th Amendment citizenship dependent on the social insurance trust, to non -14th Amendment citizens who are **self-sufficient** operating under the Public Law merchant - our nation will change - and not before.

24

Conclusion

Having been exposed to most of the information from various factions *of the "patriot" sector* on how to *get back our rights* under the Constitution, none have addressed the *real issues of law*.

The groups that are claiming victories in *their skirmishes with big brother* are not winning on *issues of law*, rather the wins are nothing more than the result of technical knockouts. Their skill at discovering *procedural fouls* of either *the rules* or *the Codes* that govern *the system that they are an intimate part of,* is the measure of their *failure or success*. Even with a legal win, under the 14th Amendment trust and its conscience, there is nothing to prevent the trust from instituting *new proceedings* at a later date. This is because the *conscience of the trust* is altered according to *expediency*. The real issues of law, that are the *foundation of our political system*, continue to be evaded by the so-called *"patriot"*.

> *"If laws are to have a binding force, it follows that, in view of the right of self-consciousness, they must be universally known ... To hang the laws so high that no citizen could read them is injustice of one and the same kind as to bury them in row upon row of learned tomes, collections of dissenting judgments and opinions, records of customs, etc., and in a dead language too, so that knowledge of the law of the land is accessible only to those who have made it their professional study."* /87

Hegel's comments are extremely appropriate for today even though they were written in the last century. What has been discovered is **comparable to revisiting** the chambers where our founding fathers met *in secret*. They purposely **disguised some of the language** in terms that would not allow tampering and loss of **basic issues of law** that are the **foundation of the Republic**. A foundation based on the **common civil law** without the **private conscience** of any **church/charitable organization**.

Yes, it is the peoples' fault - our fault for allowing a complacency about our liberty **to put us to sleep**.

In the beginning of our country, **every household studied the law as much as they studied their Bible**. They came to appreciate **knowing and using the Law** more than any modern day attorney. However, gradually the professional **attorney _at_ law** dominated the **political picture** and this led to **our lawmakers** being better informed in **private law for commercial purposes** because it was their specialty. Thus, our government and its vast majority of **private "at-law" law makers** turned its citizens into people who only knew what it was like to **operate under private church law** controlling **commercial public policy**.

This has given us a **school system, both public and private**, that is graduating students who **have no idea what the absolute freedoms of the Constitution mean**. Students are born, bred and raised on the **prejudice toward an old communal democracy** being advertised as the New World Order where **the state is sovereign** - not the individual.

From the **historical records** it is evident that our

fore-fathers knew that, at some point beyond their time, *the majority of people of this nation* would get enticed and prejudiced into an *economic jurisdiction* that would become repugnant.

The Constitution allowes those *repugnant jurisdictions* but it also made provision for one *to walk away from them* anytime he would *individually choose to do so*.

Knowing the law *will allow one to do just that* and that is what this Treatise is all about.

U.S.A. The Republic

Postscript

Most people believe that a church with a 501(c)(3) tax exemption is a "tax exempt church". They err greatly. A church with a 501(c)(3) tax exemption is *not* a "tax exempt church"... it is a tax exempt *"organization."*

A "religious or church organization" is a corporation that "functions" in a "legal capacity" doing "business" *as* a church.

The IRS is fully aware of this distinction because all of their publications reflect it. Nowhere do they refer to "tax exempt" churches. There is no such thing. They always refer to "religious or church organizations." Surely, Congress understands the distinction as well?!!

A church that voluntarily initiates an "application" to the State for "corporate status" obtains "limited liability" and "tax exemption." The church has petitioned the State to authorize it's right to prosper and exist. Thus the church consents to a "change of its status" from a "lawful assembly of private citizens" to that of a "legal government franchise" of public, 14th Amendment subjects of the State.

A true church (a congregation of believers) does not have rights granted by the Constitution. It has inalienable rights granted by God and "secured" by the Bill of Rights to the U.S. Constitution.

Incorporated "churches" and artificial "persons" (corporations) do *not* have "inalienable rights" granted by God "secured" by the Constitution. They only have rights, privileges, and immunities that are granted to entities created by the State. The U.S. Supreme Court understands that corporations are "creatures of the State"... as the U.S. Supreme Court has stated:

"A corporation is an artificial being, invisible, intangible, and existing only in contemplation of law. Being the mere creature of law, it possesses only those properties which the charter of its creation confers upon it, either expressly, or as incidental to its existence. These are such as are supposed best calculated to effect the object for which it was created. Among the most important are immortality, and, if the expression may be allowed, individuality... properties by which a perpetual succession of many persons are considered as the same... and may act as a single individual. They enable a corporation to manage its own affairs and to hold property, without endless necessity of perpetual conveyances for the purpose of transmitting it from hand to hand. It is chiefly for the purpose of clothing bodies of men with these qualities and capacities, for which corporations were invented and are in use."

Dartmouth College v. Woodward, 4 Wheat. Rep. 634,
Osborn et. al. v. The Bank of the United States, 9 Wheat 740 at 767.

"A corporation is a creature of the state. It is presumed to be incorporated for the benefit of the public. It receives certain special privileges and franchises.. . Its powers are limited by law ... Its rights to act as a corporation are only preserved to it so long as it obeys the laws of its creation."

Wilson v. U.S., 221 U.S. 382.

"... Corporations are not citizens... The term citizen ... applies only to natural persons... not to artificial persons created by the legislature..."

Paul v. Virginia, 8 Wall. 168, 177.

(*See also the Opinion of Field, J., in the Slaughter-house Cases, 16 Wall.36,99.*)

"Whenever a corporation makes a contract it is the contract of the legal entity... The only rights it can claim are the rights which are given to it in that charter, and not the

rights which belong to its members as citizens of a state."
Bank of Augusta v. Earle, 13 Pet. 586.

"A corporation can only appear by its attorney or solicitor, duly authorized; and if this authority is not apparent upon the face of the record, the decree is erroneous, and cannot be supported."
Osborn et.al. v. The Bank of the United States, 9 Wheat 740 at 767.

According to IRS Publication 557, the instruction manual for organizations seeking recognition of tax exemption under section 501(c)(3) of the Internal Revenue Code, in order to be an "organization", in the legal sense, it is necessary to incorporate.

Black's Law Dictionary, 5th Ed., defines "Organization":

"Organization includes a corporation or governmental subdivision or agency, business trust, partnership or association, two or more persons having a joint or common interest, or any other legal or commercial entity."
— *UCC 1-201(28)*

Notice that all of the entities in the definition are government franchises under the jurisdiction of the Uniform Commercial Code (UCC) which has been "Codified" into law within each state. The definition is *sound evidence* that a corporation (even if it functions as a church) is recognized by law as a commercial and public activity. An incorporated church is "legally" a commercial or public activity. Didn't Jesus say that His house was not to be a house of merchandise (commerce)?

"And [Jesus] said unto them that sold doves, Take these things hence; make not my Father's house an house of merchandise." — John 2:16.

Since incorporated churches must register with the State tax commission as an "organization," most States will not permit exempt status until the Church applies for and obtains a 501(c)(3) status ruling of the IRS. As long as the church "organization" toes the government "public policy" line, and performs according to the terms of the charter, remaining non-political and non-controversial, it retains its tax exempt status without hassle. Of course, that means that the "church" must comply with every nit-picking demand, passed by government, that applies to any public entity... including humanist doctrines of a "One World Caesar."

IRS Publication 557 stipulates that:

"Sec.508(c) of the Internal Revenue Code provides that churches are not required to apply for recognition of section 501(c)(3) status, in order to be exempt from federal taxation, or to receive tax deductible contributions.

"Churches are *automatically exempt* from Federal income tax. Contributions to churches are *deductible by donors* under section 170 of the IRS Code."

If Churches are "automatically exempt," then why would they be so naive as to *apply* for exemption? Exemption or immunity is a *government grant* afforded only to certain classes of *juristic persons.* Law Dictionaries that define "exempt" and "immune" - plus Webster's 1828 Dictionary for the word "exclude" - will provide you with a clearer understanding of what is being said here.

The First Amendment PROHIBITS government from making any law either for or against the exercise of "religion." Laws that grant special benefits *for* religion are just as bad as laws enacted *against* religion.

The free exercise clause DOES NOT make the Church "immune" or "exempt" from anything. It excludes unfranchised Churches from the "legal jurisdiction" of man, but not from the "lawful Common Law of God". A Church that fully retains its First Amendment status is "lawfully" and automatically "excluded" from any form of direct taxation or public laws governing business franchises.

When citing the First Amendment, it should be considered in all its parts, Freedom of Speech, Freedom of the Press, and Freedom of Assembly are equally as important to the Church as any other part. Any law that infringes upon the inalienable right of pastors or believers saying or teaching whatever is proper and sound according to God's word, including His commandments on the unlawfulness of homosexuality, abortion, pornography, miscegenation, taxation and evil doings of government, etc., must be considered null and void. The same holds true for the printed word. It must be concluded that for religious free exercise to exist, free choice as to whom may or may not assemble in a private setting must be upheld. A free un-incorporated Church cannot be held to the standards of a corporation doing "business" as a church.

A Church congregation is a private assembly of individuals coming together as a family or brotherhood to worship their Lord according to the dictates of their conscience. Biblical worship is not a "public" activity. Jesus Christ, not the State, ordained the assembling together of believers.

Legislatures pass laws effecting "juristic entities" as a safeguard to the "general" health, safety and welfare of the public as a whole. Congress has no authority to grant "special" benefits or privileges to un-enfranchised churches or religious activities. The IRS only authorizes such "privileged" exemptions to churches that are incorporated as organizations. When a church possesses such "benefits" it is because it has petitioned and accepted the State's franchise. As a "legal organization", the church removed itself from the protection of the First Amendment and is no longer a free entity. As a subject of Caesar, the church is rendering unto Caesar that which is God's.

It is the Church, not the State, that has transgressed the barrier separating Church and State.

The greatest single thread that binds the Church to government is the act of "incorporation."

Addendum

U.S.A. The Republic

Addemdum 1
1865 - The American Civil War

In the decades that both preceded and followed the American civil war, The Committee of 300, the Jesuits and the 13 Papal Bloodline families began an overt attempt to exert influence over, and to regain control of the United States of America. The British monarchy accomplished this in much the same way that it had previously done throughout England: Through the control of land, resources, and finances.

By aligning themselves with wealthy individuals such as J.P. Morgan, John D. Rockefeller, Andrew Mellon, Paul Warburg, and E.H. Harriman (many of whom had become quite rich through their efforts in acting as defense contractors as part of the war effort), the same scheme was enacted all over again: Accumulation of massive amounts of wealth through war, and afterwards, at the expense of slave labor, but this time in the United States. Incidentally, Morgan and Warburg were American agents of the Rothschild family back in England.

U.S.A. The Republic

13th Amendment

In the years immediately following the American Civil War, a most heinous scheme was undertaken by the British monarchy to take back control of the United States. The first step that needed to be taken was that of enacting a *coup d'etat* against the original "Constitution for the United States of America" and the original, organic 13th Amendment. The process began when, in 1865, in the immediate aftermath of the Civil War, the *currently listed* 13th Amendment, which deals with the issue of the outlaw of slavery, was passed by Congress to overwrite the *original, organic* 13th Amendment, which had been passed on May 1st, 1810, and reads as follows,

> *"If any citizen of the United States shall accept, claim, receive, or retain any title of nobility or honour, or shall without the consent of Congress, accept and retain any present, pension, office, or emolument of any kind whatever, from any emperor, king, prince, or foreign power, such person shall cease to be a citizen of the United States, and shall be incapable of holding any office of trust or profit under them, or either of them."*

The reason for the passing of the original 13th Amendment in 1810 is explained as follows by modern-day military insider Drake Bailey, who states,

"After winning our independence from Great Britain, the United States became alarmed that agents representing the interest of foreign powers were meddling in our internal affairs. International Bankers, lawyers and other opportunists were using their money to purchase special benefits and privileges from the government officials. In order to prevent the corruption, the Senate and the House approved of a 13th amendment in 1810. This Amendment prohibited government officials from taking bribes in exchange for political favors. The Amendment prohibited anyone from receiving a Title of Nobility or receiving any honor or entitlement that would not be available to all Americans. Lawyers were prohibited from serving as elected officials while they were active members of a BAR Association. The proponents of the Amendment did not believe that a Lawyer, being an officer of the Court should simultaneous serve as a member of both the Judicial and Legislative Branches of Government."

It is important to bear in mind that, while the modern-day version of the 13th Amendment seems at first glance to be an honorable attempt to end slavery America, it was in fact a blatant attempt to 'hide' and to 'suppress' the original 13th Amendment, which again, prohibited titles of nobility as well as prevented government officials from receiving any type of gift, monetary or otherwise, from a noble.

This is of vast importance when one understands that the entire history of the European world, dating back to the time of ancient Greece and Rome, has been the story of one tyrannical emperor after another, one oligarchy following the next, for thousands of years. The modern-day descendants of these ancient bloodlines still exist to this day, and assume command of the very highest levels of global control and power. The very foundations of the United States are based upon our 'breaking free' from the chains of control exerted over us by these ancient bloodline families. The following links will provide a great deal more insight into this issue.

The following article by archival researcher David M. Dodge and former police investigator Tom Dunn goes into great detail regarding the fact that the 'disappearance' of the original, organic 13th Amendment was a key phase in the silent takeover of the United States by the British monarchy.

http://www.lawfulpath.com/ref/13th-amend.shtml

U.S.A. The Republic

14th Amendment

The foundation of the United States of America was, without question, a unique historical event. One very important fact that has, to a great extent, been lost to history is that, through the wording of both the Articles of Confederation as well as the Constitution, each individual State within the union was recognized as a sovereign entity, an independent nation-state. The powers of the federal government were severely limited, and the States themselves held most of the power. Many of the original founders of the Constitution foresaw the inherent dangers in placing too much power into the hands of one central governing body, and these men took careful measures to both ensure and to protect the States' rights. Thus, it was decided by those in positions of power outside of the United States that the best way to take apart the nation was to divide it by making a covert attempt to strip away the rights of the individual nation-states and to centralize power.

In April of 1866, a 2/3 vote of both Congress and the House of Representatives allowed the passage of the Civil Right's Act, despite the bill being vetoed by President Andrew Johnson. This act by Johnson forever tarnished his name, and history has branded him a racist. In a statement made to the Senate in March of 1866, Johnson states the following:

"By the first section of the bill, all persons born in the United States, and not subject to any foreign power, excluding Indians not taxed, are declared to be citizens of the United States. This provision comprehends the Chinese of the Pacific States, Indians subject to taxation, the people called Gipsies, as well as the entire race designated as blacks, people of color, negroes, mulattoes, and persons of African blood. Every individual of these races, born in the United States, is by the bill made a citizen of the United States. It does not purport to declare or confer any other right of citizenship than Federal citizenship; it does not propose to give these classes of persons any status as citizens of States, except that which may result from their status as citizens of the United States. The power to confer the right of State citizenship is just as exclusively with the several States, as the power to confer the right of Federal citizenship is with Congress. The right of Federal citizenship, thus to be conferred in the several excepted ratios before mentioned, is now, for the first time, proposed to be given by law."

The most important thing to take away from this statement, when reading between the lines, is the fact that Johnson is telling the Senate that the language of this bill sets forth a FEDERAL citizenship status upon all natural born peoples of the United States, thus taking that right away from the States. This was a first step in a much larger plan to centralize power into the hands of the federal government.

In July of 1868, the 14th Amendment of the Constitution was 'ratified' by Congress. What many do not realize, however, is that this act was never ratified by President

Johnson, but was rather vetoed by the President. Prior to this, in 1867, Congress went outside of its Constitutional powers by declaring the first of two Reconstruction Acts, (again, vetoed by Johnson), which divided the Southern States into five separate military districts, each under the rule of a military general. This was a further extension of the state of martial law which had been declared by President Lincoln in 1863. In response to the Reconstruction Acts, Johnson stated,

> *"I have examined the bill 'to provide for the more efficient government of the rebel States' with the care and the anxiety which its transcendent importance is calculated to awaken. I am unable to give it my assent for reasons so grave that I hope a statement of them may have some influence on the minds of the patriotic and enlightened men with whom the decision must ultimately rest.*
>
> *The bill places all the people of the ten States therein named under the absolute domination of military rulers; and the preamble undertakes to give the reason upon which the measure is based and the ground upon which it is justified. It declares that there exists in those States no legal governments and no adequate protection for life or property, and asserts the necessity of enforcing peace and good order within their limits."*

Several "Governors" of the southern States were removed from Civil Office by "Military Commanders" under...Section 2 of the Reconstruction Act of July 19, 1867 and were replaced with "Army Officials" or other military appointees. These Military Commanders or appointees declared that they had the authority to reject or approve 'Resolutions' of the Legislatures of their 'Military Districts' and they declared that they had the authority to submit 'Resolutions of Ratification' to the U.S. Secretary of State declaring that the Legislatures of their 'Military Districts' had ratified the 14th and 15th Amendments to the United States Constitution. [Note: 'Military Districts' are not 'States' of the Union. 'Military Districts' are subject to the exclusive jurisdiction of the U.S. Congress while a State of the Union is a foreign corporation to the United States *(more on this in the next section) that exercises sovereign authority of its own. The two forms of government are different and they cannot co-exist. The U.S. Congress, in and through its Military Districts, has no authority to ratify Amendments to the U.S. Constitution.

As we can plainly see, the 14th Amendment of the Constitution was never ratified by the U.S. president and was passed under illegal and unconstitutional circumstances while the nation was under a state of forced martial law. In essence, what the 14th Amendment did was to change the citizenship status of all U.S. citizens, making them FEDERAL citizens as opposed to STATE citizens. This fact is of extreme importance, for as we shall see, the final 'phase' of this operation, this silent 'coup d'etat' against the original United States Constitutional Republic, was yet to come.

District of Columbia Act of 1871

The District of Columbia Act of 1871 represents the single most tyrannical action ever undertaken against the Constitution for the United States of America and its citizens.

In the aftermath of the Civil War, the nation found itself torn in two and with barely the financial means to maintain itself as a Republic. Through the illegal and unconstitutional signing of the 14th Amendment, (by military commanders under Martial Law), the citizen status of ALL U.S. citizens was changed from State to Federal.

What happened next almost defies logic, but was a scheme so clever, so deceptive, that it makes one's head spin.

With the passage of the District of Columbia Act of 1871, the Constitution for the United States of America was officially changed to the CONSTITUTION OF THE UNITED STATES OF AMERICA (*all caps*). The name of the country, as written on all legally binding documents, was changed from the United States of America to the UNITED STATES OF AMERICA (*all caps*).

This is important because as we are told by the U.S. Government Printing Office Styles Manual, ALL CAPS in a legal document signifies either a U.S. vessel, a corporation, or a debt person. What this did, (are you ready for this one), is transformed the country into a CORPORATION under the control of the British monarchy, and each and every citizen of the Republic then became a Corporate Vessel (the "ship" of your estate) with a monetary value, under the ownership of the corporation.

We were no longer seen as people, but rather we have been used as debt instruments against the overall debt of the U.S. corporation, whereby a trust fund was (and still is) set up in our names upon the time of our birth when our mother signs off on our birth certificate.

Our social security number is used as a means of setting up ten separate and distinct trust funds under the auspices of the U.S. corporation. The District of Columbia, i.e. Washington, D.C., became a completely separate entity unto itself, which became the head of this corporation. In effect, the Constitutional Republic was given a sleeping pill, and in its place was formed a CORPORATION ultimately under the control the British Monarchy and the Rothschild banking cabal.

All that we had fought for one hundred years earlier as part of the American Revolution was falsely shoved aside into the waste bin with the stroke of a pen. From this point forward, each and every single member of Congress, the House of Representatives, and the U.S. President swore an allegiance not to the Constitutional Republic, but to the CORPORATION of the UNITED STATES OF AMERICA.

This effectively labels them as traitors to the Republic and to the people of this nation, as this system of tyranny remains intact to this very day. In effect, the 'government' became the overseers of Corporation U.S.A. According to the exact wording in Chapter 62 of the Act itself,

"Be it enacted by the Senate and the House of Repre-sentatives of the United States of America in Congress assembled, That all part of the territory of the United States included within the limits of the District of Columbia be, and the same is hereby, created into a government by the name of the District of Columbia, by which name it is hereby constituted a body corpo-rate for municipal purposes."

What Congress did by passing the Act of 1871 was create an entirely new document, a constitution for the government of the District of Columbia, an INCORPO-RATED government. This newly altered Constitution was not intended to benefit the Republic. It benefits only the corporation of the UNITED STATES OF AMERICA and operates entirely outside the original (organic) Constitution.

Instead of having absolute and unalienable rights guar-anteed under the organic Constitution, we the people now have "relative" rights or privileges.

One example is the Sovereign's right to travel, which has now been transformed (under corporate government policy) into a "privilege" that requires citizens to be licensed. By passing the Act of 1871, Congress committed TREASON against the People who were Sovereign under the grants and decrees of the Declaration of Independence and the organic Constitution.

In preparation for stealing America, the puppets of Britain's banking cabal had already created a second government, a Shadow Government designed to manage what the common herd believed was a democracy, but what really was an incorporated UNITED STATES. Together this chimera, this two-headed monster, disallowed the common herd all rights of sui juris [sovereignty].

Congress, with no authority to do so, created a separate form of government for the District of Columbia, a ten-mile square parcel of land...the Civil War was, in fact, little more than a calculated front with fancy footwork by backroom players.

It was also a strategic maneuver by British and European interests (international bankers) intent on gaining a stranglehold on the coffers of America. And, because Congress knew our country was in dire financial straits, certain members of Congress cut a deal with the international bankers (in those days, the Rothschilds of London were dipping their fingers into everyone's pie)...There you have the WHY, why members of Congress permitted the international bankers to gain further control of America.

Then, by passing the Act of 1871, Congress formed a corporation known as THE UNITED STATES. This corporation, owned by foreign interests, shoved the organic version of the Constitution aside by changing the word 'for' to 'of' in the title. Let me explain: the original Constitution drafted by the Founding Fathers read: 'The Constitution for the united states of America.' [note that neither the words 'united' nor 'states' began with capital letters]. But the 'CONSTITUTION OF THE UNITED STATES OF AMERICA' is a corporate constitution, which is absolutely NOT the same document you think it is. First of all, it ended all our rights of sovereignty [sui juris]. So you now have the HOW, how the international bankers got their hands on THE UNITED STATES OF AMERICA."

Act of 1871 Review

1871, February 21: Congress Passes an Act to Provide a Government for the District of Columbia, also known as the Act of 1871.

With no constitutional authority to do so, Congress created a separate form of government for the District of Columbia, a ten mile square parcel of land (see, Acts of the Forty-first Congress," Section 34, Session III, chapters 61 and 62).

The act — passed when the country was weakened and financially depleted in the aftermath of the Civil War — was a strategic move by foreign interests (international bankers) who were intent upon gaining a stranglehold on the coffers and neck of America. Congress cut a deal with the international bankers (specifically Rothschilds of London) to incur a DEBT to said bankers.

Because the bankers were not about to lend money to a floundering nation without serious stipulations, they devised a way to get their foot in the door of the United States.

The Act of 1871 formed a corporation called THE UNITED STATES.

The corporation, OWNED by foreign interests, moved in and shoved the original Constitution into a dustbin. With the Act of 1871, the organic Constitution was defaced — in effect vandalized and sabotage — when the title was capitalized and the word "for" was changed to "of" in the title.

THE CONSTITUTION OF THE UNITED STATES OF AMERICA is the constitution of the incorporated UNITED STATES OF AMERICA. It operates in an economic capacity and has been used to fool the People into thinking it governs the Republic. It does is not!

Capitalization is NOT insignificant when one is referring to a legal document. This seemingly "minor" alteration has had a major impact on every subsequent generation of Americans. What Congress did by passing the Act of 1871 was create an entirely new document, a constitution for the government of the District of Columbia, an INCORPORATED government.

This corporation counted on the fact that most people are too indifferent, unconcerned, distracted, or lazy to learn what they need to know to survive within the system. We have been conditioned to let the government do our thinking for us. Now's the time to turn that around if we intend to help save our Republic and ourselves — before it's too late.

As an instrument of the international bankers, the UNITED STATES owns you from birth to death. It also holds ownership to all your assets, to your property, even to your children.

Think long and hard about all the bills taxes, fines, and licenses you have paid for or purchased. Yes, they have you by the pockets. If you don't believe it, read the 14th Amendment. See how 'free' you really are.

Ignorance of the facts led to your silence. Silence is construed as consent; consent to be the beneficiaries of a debt you did not incur. As a Sovereign People we have been deceived for hundreds of years; we think we are free, but in truth we are servants of the corporation.

Congress committed treason against the People in 1871.

Honest men could have corrected the treason and fraud. But apparently there weren't enough honest men to counteract the lust for money and power. We lost more freedom than we will ever know, thanks to corporate infiltration of our so-called 'government.'

Do you think that any soldier who died in any of our many wars would have fought if he or she had known the truth? Do you think one person would have laid down his/her life for a corporation? How long will we remain silent? How long will we perpetuate the MYTH that we are free? When will we stand together as One Sovereign People? When will we take back what has been as stolen from the us?

If the People of America had known to what extent their trust was betrayed, how long would it have taken for a real revolution to occur? What we now need is a Revolution in THOUGHT. We need to change our thinking, then we can change our world. Our children deserve their rightful legacy — the liberty our ancestors fought to preserve, the legacy of a Sovereign and Fully Free People.

U.S.A. The Republic

Recap

1871, February 21: Congress Passes an Act to Provide a Government for the District of Columbia, also known as the Act of 1871.

With no constitutional authority to do so, Congress created a separate form of government for the District of Columbia, a ten mile square parcel of land (see, Acts of the Forty-first Congress," Section 34, Session III, Chapters 61 and 62).

The act — passed when the country was weakened and financially depleted in the aftermath of the Civil War — was a strategic move by foreign interests (international bankers) who were intent upon gaining a stranglehold on the coffers and neck of America. Congress cut a deal with the international bankers (specifically Rothschilds of London) to Incur a DEBT to said bankers.

Because the bankers were not about to lend money to a floundering nation without serious stipulations, they devised a way to get their foot in the door of the United States.

The Act of 1871 formed a corporation called THE UNITED STATES.

The corporation, OWNED by foreign interests, moved in and shoved the original Constitution into a dustbin. With the Act of 1871, the organic Constitution was defaced — in effect vandalized and sabotage — when the title was capitalized and the word "for" was changed to "of" in the title.

THE CONSTITUTION OF THE UNITED STATES OF AMERICA is the constitution of the incorporated UNITED STATES OF AMERICA. It operates in an economic capacity and has been used to fool the People into thinking it governs the Republic. It does is not!

Capitalization is NOT insignificant when one is referring to a legal document. This seemingly "minor" alteration has had a major impact on every subsequent generation of Americans. What Congress did by passing the Act of 1871 was create an entirely new document, a constitution for the government of the District of Columbia, an INCORPOR- ATED government.

This corporation counted on the fact that most people are too indifferent, unconcerned, distracted, or lazy to learn what they need to know to survive within the system. We have been conditioned to let the government do our thinking for us. Now's the time to turn that around if we intend to help save our Republic and ourselves — before it's too late.

As an instrument of the international bankers, the UNITED STATES owns you from birth to death. It also holds ownership to all your assets, to your property, even to your children.

Think long and hard about all the bills taxes, fines, and licenses you have paid for or purchased. Yes, they have you by the pockets. If you don't believe it, read the 14th Amendment. See how 'free' you really are.

Ignorance of the facts led to your silence. Silence is construed as consent; consent to be the beneficiaries of a debt you did not incur. As a Sovereign People we have been deceived for hundreds of years; we think we are free, but in truth we are servants of the corporation.

Congress committed treason against the People in 1871.

Honest men could have corrected the treason and fraud. But apparently there weren't enough honest men to counteract the lust for money and power. We lost more freedom than we will ever know, thanks to corporate infiltration of our so-called 'government.'

Do you think that any soldier who died in any of our many wars would have fought if he or she had known the truth? Do you think one person would have laid down his/her life for a corporation? How long will we remain silent? How long will we perpetuate the MYTH that we are free? When will we stand together as One Sovereign People? When will we take back what has been as stolen from the us?

If the People of America had known to what extent their trust was betrayed, how long would it have taken for a real revolution to occur? What we now need is a Revolution in THOUGHT. We need to change our thinking, then we can change our world. Our children deserve their rightful legacy — the liberty our ancestors fought to preserve, the legacy of a Sovereign and Fully Free People.

In the simplest sense, the disappearance of the original, organic 13th Amendment, the illegal ratification of the 14th Amendment, and the passage of the District of Columbia Act of 1871 signaled the end of the legal and lawful United States Constitutional Republic and the ushering in of a de facto government, i.e. a corporation, headquartered in the District of Columbia. The UNITED STATES OF AMERICA has been as such ever since this time.

The bureaucrats who hold seats in our government, (and this goes all the way up to the office of the President), are not tasked with maintaining the welfare of the people, but rather the welfare of corporations and big banks. Yet it is important to note that the legal and lawful U.S. Constitutional Republic has not been destroyed; it is merely in a state of slumber. The lawful and constitutional 'seats of government' under the Constitutional Republic have merely been vacated, and instead replaced by seats that serve a corporation, NOT a government.

As U.S. citizens, we have every legal right to awaken our true form of government. One of the ways this can be done is through the process of declaring oneself free from this false paradigm. In essence, each and every one of us can once again declare ourselves free people in a free nation, from the U.S. corporation.

It is up to you as a free person who longs to break free from the corporate chains that bind you, to do research on this subject. The following links provide a great deal of information regarding this process. Delve further into the many hidden truths regarding this most pivotal time of our nation's history.

Links

Go here for an official copy of the District of Columbia Organic Act of 1871, which outlines the basic structure of what would become the new government of the UNITED STATES OF AMERICA, a fascist plutocracy.

http://www.newtomorrow.us/Act_of_1871.pdf

Go here to cofirm the status of the U.S. as a corporate entity in the June of 2012 lawsuit filed against the UNITED STATES DEPARTMENT OF VETERAN AFFAIRS, in which the following is listed on page one under Defendants/Respondents: UNITED STATES OF AMERICA (corporate fiduciary, contract agent of governance).

http://www.newtomorrow.us/VA_Lawsuit.pdf

Go here to access the site of *Team Law,* a consortium of legal experts who have assembled a massive database of information pertaining to this time in the nation's history. *Team Law* assists people in regaining their legal and lawful rights under the Constitutional Republic. An original copy of the District of Columbia Act, Chapter 62 (quoted above) is included under the Historical Outline section of this website.

http://teamlaw.org/

Go here to read an in-depth research article on the concept of common vs. civil law, and their importance in understanding the ramifications of the 14th Amendment and the District of Columbia Act.

http://www.soldierhugs.com/break-free-blog/

Go here to read research articles posted to the website of *Spiritual Economics Now* to gain a better understanding of the *REAL vs. the FABRICATED* systems of law and economics currently existing in our world.

http://spiritualeconomicsnow.net/?p=306
http://spiritualeconomicsnow.net/?p=75

U.S.A. The Republic

FOOTNOTES

/1. George Rapp's commune in Harmony PA. was moved to Evansville, Indiana. After a time it was sold to Robert Owen, when George Rapp moved to Economy PA, just north of Pittsburgh. The physical remains of both communes have been converted to historical sites today.

/2. Private property as meant by Fourier was in reality Quasi private (seemingly but not really) and not allodial as was established in (u)nited States of America.

/3. "An **Association** is an assemblage of persons (from four to eighteen hundred) *united voluntarily* for the purpose of prosecuting, *with order and unity,* the various branches of Industry, Art and Science, in which they engage; *and of directing their efforts, energies and talents, in the best way for the happiness and elevation of the whole.*"

/4. "... rule by the entire adult male citizen body, known to later detractors as `ochlocracy' or mob rule." — Burns, J.H., The Cambridge History of Medieval Political Thought, Cambridge University Press, 1988.

/5. Smith v Allwright, 321 U.S. 649, 88 L.Ed. 987, 64 S.Ct. 757, 151 ALR 1110, reh den 322 U.S. 769, 88 L.Ed. 1594, 64 S.Ct. 1052.

/6. Weldon, T.D., "The Vocabulary Of Politics," 1953. Weldon was a Fellow of the College and Tudor in Philosophy, Rhodes Scholar.

/7. Karl Marx, "Communist Manifesto" of 1848.

/8. Sokoloff v National City Bank of N.Y., 239 N.Y. 158, 145 N.E. 917 [1924].

/9. Article IV, Section 4 of the Constitution of the (u)nited States of America.

/10. Hale v Henkel, 201 US 43 (1905).

/11. Ruling Case Law, Vol. 5, Section II, "Adoption of English Common Law in America."

/12. Jefferson to Monroe, May 20, 1782, Jefferson Papers, IX, p. 380, Boyd Edition. excerpt from the book "The Creation Of The American Republic," 1776-1787, (p. 610) by Gordon S. Wood, 1969.

/13. Freytag v. C.I.R., 111 S.Ct. 2631 (1991).

/14. The word (u)nited, as in (u)nited States of America shows that it is not a proper noun as in the original and actual use of the word, and it is not misspelled.

/15. "A case in admiralty does not, in fact, arise under the Constitution or Laws of the United States." American Ins. Co. v Canter, 1 Pet. 511, 545 (1828).

/16. Burns, J.H., The Cambridge History of Medieval Political Thought, Cambridge University Press, 1988, pages 65-68.

/17. Rand, E.K., Founders Of The Middle Ages, (1928) Chapter 1.

/18. Black Letter Law referred to the laws of servitude to the church or king. Black was representative of the unquestioned authority of the priest's dictates.

/19. Luke v. Lyde, 2 Burr. R. 883-887.

/20. Letter to Judge John Ryler, June 17, 1812 by Thomas Jefferson.

/21. Letter to Dr. Thomas Cooper, February 10, 1814 titled "Christianity And The Common Law."

/22. Ibid.

/23. Letter - Lincoln to H.L. Pierce., 1859

/24. A **constructive trust** *is* _construed_ (_not constructed_) because of the *inferred or presumed intent* of a property owner, as distinguished from a trust based on intent *directly or clearly expressed.* A constructive trust is a *remedial device of the court for taking property from one who is contrued to have acquired or retained it wrongfully* and *vesting title in another* in order to prevent unjust enrichment. *It is not based on the intent of the parties but rather is construed by the court in order to achieve a construed equitable result.* This is precisely what the IRS or any other authority does. *They construct a trust based on your silence under executive and legislative authority* to prevent unjust enrichment upon its 14th Amendment beneficiaries.

/25. "... the Goddess Minerva ... who sprung full-grown from the brain of Jupiter, typifies the political birth of California, which became a state without probation as a territory." From March Fong Eu, Secretary of State.

/26. The common law is referred to as the "general (commercial) common law" to remind readers that, in early nineteenth century usage, "common law" was a general (commercial) common law shared by the American states rather than a common law of a particular state.

/27. Fletcher, William A., "The General Common Law and Section 34 Of The Judiciary Act Of 1789: The Example of Marine Insurance," Harvard Law Review, Vol. 97, No. 7, May 1984, page 1515.

/28. When the people lost their law by the removal of the gold standard, *they automatically were assumed to be accepting the trust relationship and its benefits.* When a private charitable trust has at least 51% of population participating, *it becomes a public trust.*

/29. Strayer, Joseph R., On The Medieval Origins Of The Modern State [1979].

/30. 78th Congress, 1st Session, Jan. 1, 1943 to March 1, 1943. Words of Mr. Edwin Arthur Hall on January 27th. This was the year that personal income taxes started.

/31. Wills, Gary, Inventing America, Jefferson's Declaration of Independence, quoted from Jefferson's Commonplace Book.

/32. Swift v. Tyson, 16 Peters 1 (1842).

/33. Erie Railroad v. Thompkins, 304 U.S. 64.

/34. Referring to the individual person or "the person."

/35. Referring to general things of possession called "the thing."

/36. Wong Kim Ark, 169 US 649.

/37. Collins, Charles Wallace, M.A., Fellow in University of Chicago, Member of the Alabama Bar, The Fourteenth Amendment And The States: A Study Of The Operation Of The Restraint Clauses Of Section One Of The Fourteenth Amendment Of The Constitution Of The United States.

/38. Washington's "Farewell Address" to the American People, September 17, 1796.

/39. 11th Congress, 3d Session, No. 294, President Madison's Objections to the Bill "Incorporating The Protestant Episcopal Church In The Town of Alexandria, In The District of Columbia," Communicated to the House of Representatives, February 21, 1811.

/40. 40th Congress, 1st Session, Ex. Doc. No. 6, House of Representatives, Protestant Church at Rome, Message from the President of the United States, March 15, 1867.

/41. A private court of the king to enforce his arbitrary proclamations and demands.

/42. A document issued from the kings court (court of chancery) to aid in enforcing its decree to bring about a change of title to real and personal property.

/43. Frommer's Washington D.C. by Rena Bulkin and Faye Hammel, page 157, [1989-1990]

/44. SUBJECT TO. Liable, subordinate, subservient, inferior, obedient to; governed or affected by; provided that; provided; answerable for. Black's Law Dict. 4th Ed.

/45. Coleman v. Miller, 307 US 433, 83 L.Ed. 1385, 122 ALR 695.

/46. Jewett v. Commissioner of Internal Revenue, (1982) 455 US 302, 311; 71 L.Ed. 170, 176; 102 S.Ct. 1082.

/47. Beys Afroyin v Dean Rusk, Secretary of State, (1967) 387 US 253, 18 L.Ed.2d 757, 762.

/48. Davis v Beason, 133 US 333, 10 S.Ct. 299, 33 L.Ed. 637.

/49. Thomas v Collins, (1945) 323 US 516, 89 L.Ed. 430, 65 S.Ct. 315.

/50. Webster's Dict. 1947.

/51. Ibid.

/52. Johnson's Universal Cyclopedia, 1891.

/53. Latin Dict.

/54. Ibid.

/55. 15 United States Statutes at Large, Ch. 249-250, pps 223-224, Section 1, R.S. 1999, 8 USC 1481.

/56. Briehl v. Dulles, 248 F2d 561, 583 at footnote 21, (1957).

/57. "This is *the greatest danger that today threatens civilization: **State intervention**.* Society will have to live *for **the government machine**.* And as, after all, *it is only a machine whose existence and maintenance depend upon the vital supports around it,* the state, after sucking out the very marrow of society, will be left bloodless, a skeleton, dead with that rusty death of machinery, more gruesome than the death of a living organism. ***The whole of life is bureaucratic**.* What results? The bureaucratization of life begins about its absolute decaying all order. *Wealth diminishes, bursts are few.* Then **the state**, *in order to attend to its own needs, forces on still more the bureaucratization of human existence [**the militarisms of society**].*" Gasset, J. Ortega, **The Revolt Of The Masses**, [1932] page 132-133 (Excerpt from Political Institutions, A Preface page 56 [1938] by Edward McChesney Sait, Professor of Political Science, Pomona Collage)

/58. Ibid.

/59. "Democracy," from Dictionary Of The History of Ideas, Vol. 1, 1973

/60. Funk v U.S., 290 U.S. 371 (1933)

/61. Wheaton v. Peters, 8 Pet. 591

/62. Political Commerce is also referred to as the "Private Law Merchant."

/63. Swift v. Tyson, 16 Peters 1 (1842).

/64. Civil Commerce is also referred to as "Public Law Merchant."

/65. Clearfield Trust v. United States, 318 U.S. 363, 63 S.Ct. 573.

/66. There were many influential Americans who were interested in Owen's "New View of Society." Among those were Chancellor James Kent who wrote Commentaries on American Law. Jonathan Mayhew Wainwright, Bishop of Grace Church of New York, John McVickar of Columbia University, David Golden former Mayor of New York City, Supreme Court Justice Joseph Story. All had talks with Owen on his communitarian ideas. Later Owen was granted the Hall of Representatives in the Capitol for presenting his ideas. First time by Henry Clay the speaker, and second by President John Quincy Adams, Ex-President James Monroe, members of the cabinet, the Supreme Court and the Congress.

/67. The common law, as referred to here, had to do with the body of those principles and rules of action, relating to the government and security of persons and property, which derive their authority solely from usages and customs of immemorial antiquity or from the judgments and decrees of the courts recognizing, affirming, and enforcing such usages and customs, and in this sense, particularly the ancient unwritten law of England. 15A C.J.S.

/68. Erie Railroad v. Tompkins, 304 U.S. at 64 (1938).

/69. Stanek v. White, 172 Minn. 390, 215 N.W. 784.

/70. Clearfield Trust v. United States, 318 U.S. 363, 63 S.Ct. 573.

/71. See Public Law 88-243-244, 77 Stat. 630-775, 88th Congress, 1st Session, December 30, 1963.

/72. Res Lat. The subject matter of a trust or Will. In civil law, a thing; an object. As a term of the law, this word has a very wide and extensive signification, including not only things which are objects of property, but also such as are not capable of individual ownership. By res, according to the modern civilians, is meant everything that may form an object of rights, in opposition to persona, which is regarded as a subject of rights. It is everything that may form an object of rights and includes an object, subject-matter or status. In re Riggle's Will, 11 A.D.2d 51, 205 N.Y.S.2d 19-22.

/73. American Law And Procedure, page 186.

/74. This includes all the debt of bankruptcy that takes place in this country. As this treatise was receiving last minute changes, the national news broadcast the story of the largest corporate bankruptcy that has ever been filed. The company is Olympia and York. They have an estimated debt of 18 billion dollars. All the 14th Amendment citizens are going to have the privilege of helping cover the part of the 18 billion that affects the public social trust.

/75. "The Exercise Of Jurisdiction In Rem To Compel Payment Of Debt.", Harvard Law Review, Vol. XXVII., No. 2., December, 1913.

/76. "Public Policy" mutable by will as spoken of in Funk v. United States, 290 U.S. 371.

/77. Hanson v. Denckla, 357 U.S. 235 (1958).

/78. Civilly dead: dead in the view of the law; the condition of one who has lost his civil rights and capacities, and is accounted dead in law.

/79. Not being subject to the 14th Amendment and its tax codes can reduce the loss of value of your money, because you are not losing it to the trust.

/80. Alan Greenspan (1962), Chairman of the Federal Reserve Bank. Source Remnant Review, Newsletter, (June 16, 1989).

/81. Rights that cannot be taken from you or transferred to another by government. You can, however, give these Rights up of your own free will without government interference.

/82. Wills, Gary, Inventing America, Jefferson's Declaration of Independence, quoted from Jefferson's Commonplace Book, pages 142-47.

/83. Supreme Court in its usage here is not capitalized, as in the original Constitution, to show that it is functioning as an Article III court.

/84. Peter v. Peter, 343 Ill 493, 175 NE 846, 75 ALR 890; People v. Flamagin, 331 Ill 203, 162 NE 848, 60 ALR 305; Mackey v. Bowen, 332 Mass. 167, 124 NE2d 254; Garfield v. White, 326 Mass 20, 92 NE2d 575; Perkins v. Isley, 224 NC 793, 32 NE2d 588; Bacon v. Barber, 110 Vt 280, 6 A2d 9, 123 ALR 253.

85. To function "in law" means to function where the courts reveal your position in the Law which is not restrictive, because they are involved with promoting and expanding your unalienable rights by way of constitutional mandate.

/86. To function at law and its equity means to function where the courts declare the law which is the will of the legislature in trust with the person. It is restrictive in nature, because there is no constitutional mandate due to the fact that it operates outside the Constitution.

/87. Hegel's Philosophy of Right, page 215.

1. **Nesara I**
   https://www.createspace.com/3676730
2. **Nesara II**
   https://www.createspace.com/3694967
3. **Be The One**
   https://www.createspace.com/3921716
4. **Commercial Redemption**
   https://www.createspace.com/3397150
5. **Hardcore Redemption-in-Law**
   https://www.createspace.com/3475497
6. **Commercial Law Applied**
   https://www.createspace.com/3960715
7. **The Matrix As It Is**
   https://www.createspace.com/3495158
8. **Give Yourself Credit**
   https://www.createspace.com/3462990
9. **From Debt To Prosperity**
   https://www.createspace.com/3485734
10. **DebtOcracy**
    https://www.createspace.com/3650756
11. **Asset Protection**
    https://www.createspace.com/3700522
12. **Untold History Of America**
    https://www.createspace.com/3407070
13. **New Beginning Study Course**
    https://www.createspace.com/3412422
14. **Reclaim Your Sovereignty**
    https://www.createspace.com/3418256
15. **Oil Beneath Our Feet**
    https://www.createspace.com/3420496
16. **The People's Voice**
    https://www.createspace.com/3724222
17. **My Home Is My Castle**
    https://www.createspace.com/3464566
18. **Maine Street Miracle**
    https://www.createspace.com/3397262